Praise for

Reinvent the Wheel: How Top Leaders Leverage Well-Being for Success

"Each of us is shaped by our own life's journey and yet we all have one thing in common...the human experience. The journey of self-discovery and living a life filled with joy is enabled through human connection and a focus on well-being. With *Reinvent the Wheel*, Megan shares a gift of discovery that can lead to a more joyful life."

—Kevin Johnson, CEO,
Starbucks Coffee Company

"Too many people think of personal growth and career success as separate objectives when, in fact, they are closely related. *Reinvent the Wheel* provides a great guide to embracing personal growth as a way to improve success is every aspect of your life."

—John Wookey, former EVP Industry Applications,
Salesforce.com and former EVP Development, SAP

"In *Reinvent the Wheel*, Megan masterfully shows us that we can change ourselves from the inside out. Step by step, she shows us that when we prioritize our well-being, when we are mindful and have compassion for ourselves, we rise."

—Scott Shute, Head of Mindfulness and
Compassion Programs, LinkedIn

"Have you ever read a book you couldn't put down? Well, *Reinvent the Wheel* is that book. It is so interesting, inspiring, and useful, you'll be forever glad you picked it up. Its innovative insights will change the way you perceive stress and well-being, and convince you to start taking better care of yourself, your career and your loved ones…now, not someday."

—Sam Horn, CEO of the Intrigue Agency; bestselling author of
SOMEDAY is Not a Day in the Week

"Megan provides a framework for achieving the most out of one's potential by focusing on taking care of ourselves and the often dismissed notion of nutrition, rest, exercise, and spiritual renewal—all lessons I learned later than I would have liked."

—John W. Thiel, former Vice Chairman, Global Wealth &
Investment Management, Bank of America,
and former Head of Merrill Lynch Wealth Management;
Partner, My Next Season

"Incredible. Megan has created one of the most comprehensive models of what total well-being looks like. If you want to have vibrant well-being, with the body, mind and spirit all working together, this is the woman to go to."

—Jack Canfield, CEO Canfield Training Group; *New York Times*
bestselling author of *The Success Principles* and
originator of the *Chicken Soup for the Soul* series

"Megan is a passionate advocate for her health. Her positive attitude has been a huge inspiration and a catalyst for her overall well-being."

—Pedram Fatehi, MD, Medical Director,
Stanford University Health Care; Clinical Associate
Professor Medicine-Nephrology, Pulmonary &
Critical Care, Stanford School of Medicine

"Megan offers a whole-picture view of well-being and success–who embodies that more than her?—and she inspires all of us to reach higher."

—Dr. Sisa Ngebulana, CEO of Billion Group;
CEO Rebosis Property Fund Ltd.;
Director and Chairman,
New Frontier Properties Ltd.

"The goal is to be both wealthy and healthy—but is that combination actually possible? Megan McNealy shows us that it is. By weaving her own remarkable story of resilience with lessons learned from top business leaders, she masterfully disrupts the common belief that success can only be achieved at the cost of personal well-being. There truly is a better way, and this book shows us how.

—Laura Putnam, author of *Workplace Wellness That Works* and CEO of Motion Infusion

"A timely and relevant read for those of us who may not be as resilient and resourceful as Megan. It's a timeless message that good whole person health and well-being define one's success, however measured. With this book, Megan will become an inspiring and insightful leader in the wellness space."

—Jim Purcell, Founder, Returns on Well-Being;
former CEO Blue Cross & Blue Shield Rhode Island

"Megan McNealy is a wonderful storyteller, and these stories are like a breath of fresh oxygen, inspiring the reader with confidence and purpose, and exceptional models of achievement and fulfillment."

—Robert Morgan, author of *New York Times* bestseller and
Oprah Book Club Selection, *Gap Creek*;
Kappa Alpha Professor of English,
Cornell University

"*Reinvent the Wheel* is must-reading for every high-performer. Drawing upon the proven practices of today's most productive leaders, Megan McNealy gives you a personalized blueprint to increase your energy, improve your health, and rediscover a new zest for life and work. Read this book if you want to feel great and do great at the same time."

—Steve Harrison, Cofounder National Publicity
Summit, Quantum Leap, Bestseller Blueprint;
Co-owner Bradley Communications Corp.

"*Reinvent the Wheel* is a must-read for business professionals and entrepreneurs who need to pay attention to their well-being while pursuing a successful career. Many of us have put our best health on the back burner and Megan illustrates clearly through her personal experience why it is important to make it a priority. We only get one life; let's make the best of it! You are on your way to better habits once you read this compelling and interesting book."

—L. Lee Richter, Founder and CEO Richter Communications;
Award-Winning Author; Serial Entrepreneur; Mentor

"If you want to get the most out of yourself and your team, there's something more critical than higher pay, greater motivation, or the latest productivity training and that secret is what you're holding in your hands right now. If you don't give yourself and your team the right support, performance will be on a steady decline and it won't be noticeable until it's too late. This book is the antidote to the secret killer of many businesses. I give it my highest recommendation."

—Christian Mickelsen, CEO of Future Force Inc. and #1 bestselling
author of *Abundance Unleashed: Open Yourself To More
Money, Love, Health, and Happiness Now*

Reinvent the Wheel

How Top Leaders Leverage
Well-Being for Success

Megan McNealy

n_b_

NICHOLAS BREALEY
PUBLISHING

BOSTON • LONDON

First published in 2019 by Nicholas Brealey Publishing
An imprint of John Murray Press

An Hachette UK company

24   23   22   21   20   19   1   2   3   4   5   6 7   8   9   10

A CIP catalogue record for this title is available from the British Library

Library of Congress Control Number: 2019935223

ISBN 978-1-52937-474-2
US eBook ISBN 978-1-52937-473-5
UK eBook ISBN 978-1-52937-471-1

Printed and bound in the United States of America.

John Murray Press policy is to use papers that are natural, renewable, and
recyclable products and made from wood grown in sustainable forests.
The logging and manufacturing processes are expected to conform to the
environmental regulations of the country of origin.

John Murray Press Ltd   Nicholas Brealey Publishing
Carmelite House   Hachette Book Group
50 Victoria Embankment   53 State Street
London EC4Y 0DZ   Boston, MA 02109, USA
Tel: 020 3122 6000   Tel: (617) 263 1834

www.nbuspublishing.com

This book is not intended as a substitute for professional medical advice. The
reader should regularly consult a physician in all matters relating to his/her
health.

To my daughters,

Madeline and Amelia:

Our unconditional love is the greatest gift.

CONTENTS

INTRODUCTION: JUMPSTART

"The real secret of power is the consciousness of power."[1]

—Charles Haanel

WHY YOU NEED THIS BOOK

Let me ask you a question. What is more important to you right now: Doing well at work, or taking care of your well-being? That is, *doing* well or *being* well?

Did I hear you gulp? Don't worry. Most high achievers I meet, if they are honest, admit the former.

Let me ask you another question: Do you think that approach is sustainable? That is, doable in the long term?

Did you gulp again and silently say no? I get it. Many of us, deep down, know the truth that we are perilously powering along. We are beacons of excellence, and driving ourselves so hard that it's only a matter of time. We are on an unstable tightrope, with striving pulling us to one side, stress yanking us to the other, our intoxicating success tugging to the right, our imminent burnout tugging to the left.

As I said, you are not alone.

Consider the following:

- There is a huge number of us achievers—millions of people at every level of enterprise, from top executives to the general workforce—who want to attain excellence and well-being simultaneously but feel that it might be an impossibility.

- Working unsustainably hard has become a cultural badge of honor. In a *New York Times* article titled "In Silicon Valley, Working 9 to 5 Is for Losers," the writer highlights a workaholic culture where "to succeed you must be willing to give up everything."[2] Sound familiar? This isn't the only industry.

- The issue is worldwide. In the United Kingdom, a study revealed that 59 percent of employees said work is by far the most common cause of stress; the results pointed to hugely damaging effects on morale, productivity, and sickness.[3] In Japan, they even have a word for death by overworking: *karoshi.*

- It is estimated that stress is costing employers approximately $500 billion annually in absenteeism, reduced productivity, and employee turnover.[4] You may be seeing the effect in your own company.

- Medical articles linking stress and illness are becoming more widely circulated and respected, such as Mayo Clinic's article "Chronic Stress Puts Your Health at Risk"[5] and the National Institute for Occupational Safety and Health's "Workplace Stress Report."[6]

- Illnesses aggravated by stress are on the rise. According to the Center for Disease Control, in 2018 high blood pressure affected 1 in 3 adults, or 75 million Americans.[7] I know many executives who have a blood pressure cuff in their desk drawer! Autoimmune disorders, more than 80 types of which are also considered stress-aggravated, affect an estimated 50 million Americans.[8]

Are these high-performing executives, entrepreneurs, and change makers outwardly successful? Almost always.

Masters of total well-being? Vibrantly healthy and truly happy? Hardly ever.

Is there a solution to this conundrum? Absolutely YES. Interested? You've come to the right place. This entire guidebook is the solution. I believe in divine timing, and here you are.

This book will forever change your view about total well-being and standout success. It contains a completely revolutionary message about the well-being of your body, mind, and spirit and its connection to peak performance. It's the place to start, the complete program, and the ongoing lifestyle: the alpha and the omega. Like the opening quote from Charles Haanel, which refers to the "consciousness of power," your new knowledge will effect a profound, permanent change on your well-being, your personal success, and your business success, and you'll never be able to go back. You won't want to. Consider these questions:

Do you want increasingly vibrant health?
Do you want to experience more passion and joy?
Are you ready to reap the rewards of peak performance in your career?

I thought so. I am right there with you. Get ready to up-level everything.

MY STORY: YOU CAN'T CATCH A FALLING KNIFE

I smiled nervously as my martial arts teacher motioned for me to come to the center of the dojo mat by myself. He directed me to begin to demonstrate my thoroughly practiced Kung Fu techniques for my Belt Advancement Test. I knew he would be looking for total mastery, agility, and a profound amount of focused energy.

Martial arts techniques are a series of choreographed moves that you power-out full force in the air on a pretend attacker. I started with my best *Striking Asp*, a sword hand shot, a wind up above my head and sudden slash. My *Crash of the Eagle* could have been a bit sharper, but I was moving quickly, not wanting to forget the sequence. I did a back fist, not even self-conscious anymore. I felt strong, with my body doing exactly what I wanted it to. I was on fire!

My daughters, 12 and 14 years old, watched from the edge of the mat, hands in nervous fists, rooting for me. They had also put in hours upon hours of practice and were getting ready to be tested next.

Half an hour later, the three of us had achieved our much-coveted yellow belts, only the second level out of 10, but it could have been solid gold; we were so proud of each other. That my girls and I could experience this moment of triumph together—that we all had advanced—pushed us over the edge of excitement. We drove home from the dojo with the car windows open, blasting music, waving the belts like flags, high fiving, and laughing. Team Triumph.

I couldn't remember the last time my heart was beating with so much joy. I felt so alive.

Have you ever had one of these moments, where you feel so completely alive? The vibration is like a huge, brilliant balloon rising up from the party to celebrate who you really are—and who you've become.

It had been quite a long road for me. Exactly 12 years earlier, when my doctor first diagnosed my painful symptoms as rheumatoid arthritis (RA), it deflated me like a balloon, with the air suddenly and sharply gone. I sat in the examining room chair, hunched over, and when I looked toward him, I could see only his hands, explaining. He was right that all the signs were there: my hands and knees were suddenly and symmetrically painful every morning, and my blood work showed that my inflammation markers were much higher than normal. He explained that an autoimmune disease like RA occurs where your body mistakenly attacks *itself*—in this case, your joints.

The doctor declared I had a moderate-to-severe case of the disease. Then he shared both good news and bad news: there were lots of powerful and well-researched drugs to treat the pain, but it was incurable, and at this rate, I would likely be bedridden someday.

But I had been doing so well! My wealth management business at a major Wall Street firm had been successful from the start. I was tagged as an early success story, a huge honor in a business with an 80- to 90-percent failure rate for new advisors, and I was asked to speak around the United States to my peers. Adding to that, I had a toddler and a new baby, plus a successful executive husband. Two weeks prior, before my hands had started hurting, I was even offered a side hustle as a Friday tennis pro at the country club in our small town. I really had been doing so well.

In the weeks that followed, I could hardly believe how my body reacted. The tops of my hands became so swollen they were like rounded, reddish turtle shells, with the fingers totally frozen open in pain. Forget even holding a pen. I hid my hands under the conference room tables at business meetings, and for the next two full years, I had to memorize everything clients said to me.

With my hands inoperable, I had to use my forearms to pick up my little girls to hug them. If I played on the floor with them, I could not rise without help. Unable to tie shoes, I made sure the girls had shoes with Velcro straps, but I could barely handle that. Tears often poured down my face as I got them ready every morning. Forget tennis.

Have you heard the saying "You can't catch a falling knife"? Advisors use it in the financial world to encourage clients to take action. This phrase refers to an investment, or even the stock market, in freefall. It describes an out-of-control, deteriorating situation, and it speaks to a futile feeling that, propelled by downward momentum, things seem out of your hands. In every sense, my rheumatoid arthritis was a falling knife I couldn't stop. I kept my secret largely to myself, not wanting to show a weakness at work and feeling ashamed that as brilliant as I was business-wise, I could not get a handle on my health.

Even with the disease, I continued doing so well at my career. I gathered awards on my wall and achieved title after title. I added amazing wealth management clients in the senior executive niche. One year, my firm featured me in an internal training video focused on a specific and perfectly executed personal business success. The next year, I gave the keynote address at the company's Northern California yearly kickoff meeting, with hundreds of my advisor peers and even our CEO in the audience. Getting ready for the speech, I could barely get my high heels onto my swollen feet, but afterwards I remember the electrifying applause, the smiles, the congratulations, and the admiration.

Even so, the falling knife was right there, a constant reminder.

After that rousing keynote presentation, I sat in my car in the parking garage, ready to go home. Because my hands were frozen open—and extra painful from the high adrenaline and stress of the day—I managed to get the key into the ignition slot, but could not turn it. I could not start the car. I tried turning the key using *both* stiff hands, but I couldn't torque it hard enough or fast enough. I tried using my forearms, but the steering column was in the way. It was that bad. I just sat there and cried.

Over the next few years, doctors offered me 32 different prescriptions, and that wasn't counting the shots I gave myself weekly or, eventually, the IV treatments I received every six months. Even with the medication, my inflammation markers rose dangerously high, and I could not sleep more than three hours at a time without being woken by the pain. I had no idea at the time that my falling knife would have so much downward momentum: that there were additional health issues for me to deal with simultaneously, including a diagnosis of chronic kidney disease and, a few years later, a diagnosis of kidney cancer.

I am sure you know that falling knives can come in many forms. While mine happened to be huge health challenges, other difficulties could include issues with an aging parent, a troubled teenager, a pending divorce, or any hugely stressful situation. How do you turn around falling knives like this? How do you contain them safely? I have learned that the best answer is with *well-being*.

From that first day in the doctor's office years ago to today, I have been on a hero's journey to turn around my well-being: body, mind, and spirit. The good news is that I figured well-being out—what it means, what it looks like, and how to achieve it. It took 12 years of struggling through pain every single day before I finally said goodbye to rheumatoid arthritis, and two years for the chronic kidney disease to disappear into remission. It took one month for the cancer to vanish.

I no longer suffer from any of these diseases. I triumphed!

I took photos with each of my doctors on the day they discharged me, with my smile as wide as it's ever been. As much as I appreciated their care, I told them I hoped to never see them again, and I couldn't wait to run out the door.

During my healing quest, I also discovered something totally unexpected and amazing. At first, I assumed that my behind-the-scenes well-being project would derail my work success. That turned out to be totally untrue. As I began to implement my vibrant well-being strategies, my wealth management business began to thrive even more.

In 2010, in what I would describe as my worst "health storm" (and also, the year of my divorce), I went all-in on my well-being project, and guess what? Every year since 2010 has set a personal business record for me. Every year, I have done better than the year before. Between 2010 and 2018, I more than quadrupled my income.

Given the severity of my health issues, how is that simultaneous career success even possible? I didn't add a teammate, work extra hours or hire at-home help. I don't have a nanny, a mother's helper, or a house husband. I am a single mom of two teenage daughters, one of whom has an intellectual disability.

I want you to really get this. The only thing I did differently is that behind the scenes, in my free time, I made well-being my priority. It was a choice that saved my life AND catapulted my career. I inadvertently discovered that *vibrant well-being and peak performance are undeniably connected.*

Thrilled with my discovery about this powerful correlation, I began testing my theory on other achievers. Was it just me? Or were there other high performers who were powering themselves from a core of well-being?

At a dizzying speed, for the past two years, I have been interviewing CEOs and high-level senior corporate executives, successful entrepreneurs, and astonishing change-makers who embody well-being, and in every case, they gave me real-life stories and evidence of how well-being has driven their success and up-leveled their careers to heights they never thought possible. There's a surprising trend afoot.

Inspired? Want to know what this means for you? Let's go.

THREE SURPRISING TRUTHS AND THREE PROMISES

What can you expect from this guidebook in your hands? In a condensed, direct, and efficient manner (because that's what high performers want, right?), this will bring you knowledge, wisdom, clarity, and real-life and easy-to-implement strategies, all of which will up-level your personal and business success.

I want to share a real gem—an absolute truth—with you right up front here. On my journey, as you can probably guess from my harrowing health story, I learned:

Truth #1: TOTAL WELL-BEING is the most valuable asset you have.

We talk a lot about assets in the financial services business. An asset is something that you have of worth, something that you gather, a deposit into a positive future vision you want to create.

Total well-being, as the most valuable asset you have, is the power center from which everything else flows. I learned this during the four days I spent post-surgery in the UCSF Bakar Cancer Hospital. If you don't have your asset of well-being, then you can't enjoy any of your other valued assets: your money, love, nature, relationships, children, pets, hobbies, or much of anything else, either. I was stuck up there helplessly looking out the window at the view.

But what does total well-being really look like? In these pages, I will offer you both a definitive definition and a visual representation. And what does that mean for you?

Promise #1: YOU will master the concept of TOTAL
WELL-BEING and customize a plan exactly right for YOU.

Right here, right up front, I want to share with you my masterpiece, the starting point of your well-being mastery, my game-changing creation, a single image that encompasses what total well-being looks like: my Well-Being Wheel.

Why did I create this? I created it to help heal myself. Over the course of 12 years, I created this wheel by first taking a hard look at every bad habit I had, every food I was eating, every thought I was thinking, every action I was taking, every person I was interacting with, and every weakness I had (because Lord knows I was dropping fast). Then, I started actively doing the actionable opposite.

The Well-Being Wheel is the culmination of those actionable opposites, and very importantly, my meetings with dozens of traditional doctors and alternative medicine practitioners, my research, my notes from reading dozens of health-related books, my definite results, the actions that worked, my solutions, and how I brought myself back to vibrant well-being. This is the perfect-sense protocol that I wish someone had handed me back then, when I was silently suffering, holed up in my house secretly trying to find answers.

This is my gift to you. I *reinvented the wheel* for you so you don't have to!

THE WELL-BEING WHEEL

This Well-Being Wheel brought me from unspeakable suffering to complete triumph. I tried dozens and dozens of strategies for well-being, but these were the ones that worked and made the biggest impact. When they magically fit into the symmetrical Well-Being Wheel framework, I knew I had something inspired, something real and life-changing to share with you.

The good news is that no matter where your well-bring meter is right now—fabulously vibrant or depressingly dismal—you will skillfully be able to use this iconic image as a tool to up-level your well-being. I will teach you how.

Are you solutions-focused? I thought so. Me too.

Let's take an introductory tour of this Well-Being Wheel. This is just for a broad stroke, a beginning explanation. One purpose of the book is to develop this concept fully.

First, note that YOU are at the very center, divided into the core BODY, MIND, and SPIRIT aspects of YOU.

Note that there are six universal spokes radiating out from the BODY category, six from the MIND category, and six from the SPIRIT category. In my vision and belief, each of these 18 spokes *matters*. Each is weighted equally; each can elevate your well-being; and conversely, the lack of any of them could throw off the symmetry of the wheel, of your well-being, and of your best self. This is somewhat like our widely accepted financial planning concept of diversification: it's wise to spread out well-being into different spokes, all of which provide value, all of which reduce risk, and all of which, combined, give you more power.

The Well-Being Wheel spokes are universal because these broad actions would really help anyone. They are undeniably beneficial. Take a quick glance. Can we agree that generally speaking, the advice to get enough sleep and hydrate would help *anyone* on this planet who has a human body? Of course! That's what I mean. While some of them may seem vague now, I will be explaining each one and its importance in later chapters. In fact, each spoke represents a chapter in this book. How convenient is that?

The Well-Being Wheel spokes are also customizable. Customization is actually the secret sauce of my work. No question, each of us benefits from each of the 18 universal spokes of the Well-Being Wheel, but here's the rub: to really work, this wheel has to be customized for YOU.

Each of us has a unique and optimal well-being blend of BODY, MIND, and SPIRIT practices that must be custom-tailored to our specific body and situation. It's the same situation with cars. We all know that, in general, all cars need certain elements to run optimally, like frequent oil changes and wheel rotations. However, we also know that you don't service a Ford F-150 the same as a Formula One car. That's obvious. Same with people.

Together, we are going to address all of the universal BODY, MIND, and SPIRIT spokes, and then actively figure out what your optimal customizations are. No two customized Well-Being Wheels are alike because no two people are alike.

Armed with your customized Well-Being Wheel, you will be able to take very specific action steps to improve every aspect of your BODY, MIND, and SPIRIT. These combined custom-tailored practices (circling around the wheel) can unleash your immense personal power so that you can experience your highest potential and live with greater health, vibrancy, and happiness. To my delight, after adopting this approach, I found myself to be better than ever, in an even more powerful racecar. You will too.

As you know from my story, I originally assumed that my well-being quest would derail my career, but the opposite happened. My second learned truth—one of the greatest discoveries in my entire life and a total game-changer—is this:

Truth #2: Well-being DRIVES success, and because of that Well-Being = Wealth-Being.

I am here to tell you that you don't have to choose between DOING well and BEING well ever again. No one in the business world *ever* says this. Let's let that sink in for a moment.

I am here to tell you that *how you spend your off-work time directly and profoundly impacts your in-work performance, productivity, and success.* How you spend your free time can absolutely help you amass power to achieve the things you want in life.

In fact, the opposite is true too. Total lack of well-being—destructive behaviors behind the scenes—can cost you business, the ability to close that sale, and, essentially, money.

Most of the workforce worldwide mistakenly believes that well-being will come after success, when you have the time and money to focus on it. Nothing could be further from the truth. The truth is that total well-being drives, promotes, and accelerates success, perfect health, joy, optimal productivity, and peak performance in business and in life.

Promise #2: Knowing HOW and WHY well-being drives success, you will become a master of well-being and wealth-being.

To show you how and why well-being drives success, I placed some revolutionary additions on my original Well-Being Wheel. I call this souped-up version the Wealth-Being Wheel—a single image that shows what total well-being looks like plus the positive outcomes for someone personally *and* professionally.

THE WEALTH-BEING WHEEL

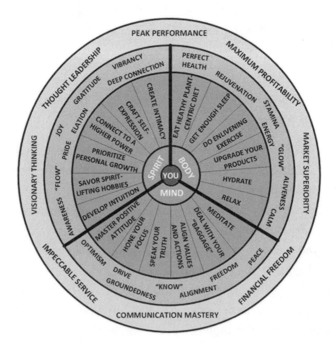

Even as a professional wealth management advisor, I consider wealth to be much, much more than money. You probably do too. I consider wealth to include personal abundance and happiness as well as career peak performance and prosperity. You can see our original Well-Being Wheel in the center, and these two added rings surrounding the wheel show a plethora of valued outcomes.

Focus on the first inner ring that circles the universal spokes, the one that looks like a bike wheel. These are the direct results, the positive personal outcomes from a powerful mastery of those nearby BODY, MIND, and SPIRIT spokes. We are strivers motivated by results, and who wouldn't be motivated by these? Every one of them is an incredible future outcome, a huge win! See, for instance, that for the BODY category, having mastery of the *Get Enough Sleep* spoke would result in rejuvenation. Having mastery of *Prioritize Personal Growth* leads to pride. You are training your eye outward.

Lastly, focus on the very outer ring that circles the universal spokes and the positive personal outcomes. This is the business success ring, or the positive professional outcomes. As you can see, and will begin to fully understand, these outcomes originate from well-being and produce results like peak performance, impeccable service, and communication mastery. I have these business outcomes flexibly floating in the outer ring because the benefits from the well-being spokes contribute to them all collectively. I can't think of a single executive or entrepreneur who wouldn't welcome the lineup in this outer circle. Is there anything there that wouldn't thrill you? I want it all too!

As I mentioned in my story, I became hugely interested in learning if and how other senior leaders were leveraging well-being to drive success. My career-long target market for my wealth management business is senior corporate executives, and I started inquiring and researching.

I used to think that the most impressive leaders in the world were driven by intelligence, drive, and excellence. This *is* true on many levels. For those of you who still may have some reservations, I uncovered some surprising news for you:

*Truth #3: The most impressive leaders in the world
are powered by Well-Being and Wealth-Being.*

I discovered a new type of leader who has emerged among us, fueled by *well-being and wealth-being*, and inspiring beyond belief. I call them Exceptional Executives, and they are a new generation of top leaders and entrepreneurs who are amassing power with their behind-the-scenes well-being and leading some of the most successful companies in the world. My focus and research these past two years has been uncovering their daily strategies and practices to find out how they show up with so much power.

Remember how I started with the incredible Charles Haanel quote, "The real secret of power is the consciousness of power"? I want your awareness to be heightened, for your new knowledge to be nailed down so that you really know. The best way to do that is to give you some living proof, besides myself!

*Promise #3: Incredible, inspiring well-being
customizations from these Exceptional Executives.*

In a corporate culture that rarely takes a break for lunch, these Exceptional Executives confidently manage their well-being to perfection, using exactly the same universal strategies I used to heal myself, to boost my career to new heights. These outrageously powerful leaders are fueled by *well-being*, leading our most cutting-edge companies from that center of power. Like me, and like you very soon, they have unique customizations that are ideal for them, and they know that their strategies deliver like nothing else. They are living examples of each spoke in glorious action! I interviewed each of these titans personally—one of the great honors of my life—and as a result I have some original, incredible, and surprising stories to share with you. Masters of their free time, beacons of self-care, doing what they love and what fuels them, they prioritize their custom Well-Being Wheels so rigorously and execute them so impressively that they show up to work and to their lives in breakout mode. I am going to take you into their worlds, where you will learn things like the favorite breakfast ritual of John Mackey, the Cofounder and CEO of Whole Foods Market; why a good festival inspires Chip Conley, a serial entrepreneur; or the secrets to staying focused by Robyn Denholm, CFO of Telstra and the Chairman of the Board of Tesla. I guarantee that you will be uplifted by the behind-the-scenes strategies of the 18 jaw-dropping leaders in this book—and perhaps inspired to take on some of their innovative ideas for yourself!

I will let you in on two unexpected and surprising secrets about these Exceptional Executives as a group right up front:

- They don't waste time, and well-being *saves* them time.
- They leverage their free time to amass personal and business power.

I will show you exactly how the Exceptional Executives accomplish this. Their stories will convince you unequivocally that well-being does drive, promote, and accelerate success, and they will inspire you tenfold to launch your own customized well-being strategy.

As billionaire investing icon Warren Buffett has said, "Ultimately, there's one investment that supersedes all others: Invest in yourself."[9] I couldn't agree more, and I bet they all would too. Welcome to the club.

A GUIDEBOOK FOR YOU

Reinvent the Wheel contains everything I wish I had known back then. It would have saved me years of suffering. I hope it prevents you from suffering from here on out.

This material continues to serve as my most valued, critical resource even now that I am radiating with vibrant health. It is designed for you, from now on, to dive right in to whichever spoke chapter calls you, wherever your interest leads. For that reason, it is intentionally not written in chronological order. Every spoke matters, and one doesn't build on the next. The spokes all stand on their own. High achievers tend to flip ahead to what interests them. You have my full permission.

Reinvent the Wheel is presented with the hope that it motivates you to do things differently. That instead of burning out and crashing down, you rise up and experience the highest levels of health, happiness, personal achievement, and business success you've ever dreamed of. The remarkable good news is that it is *all* sourced from the same power center, and it's all just a huge, rising tide.

Are you ready to get started? Like the night when my girls and I passed our Belt Advancement Test at our martial arts studio, I feel so alive. I am waving my belt of solid gold, celebrating the YOU who is about to up-level everything.

—Megan McNealy, San Francisco, 2019

PART ONE

Universal BODY Spokes

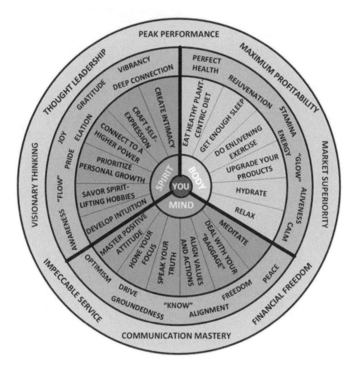

Eat a Healthy, Plant-Centric Diet: Rainbow Food on Planes

"Your fork, the most powerful tool to transform your health and change the world."[1]

—Mark Hyman, MD

RAINBOW SPRINKLE DONUTS

If you head into the employee break room at my top Fortune 500 company today, there's a very good chance you will see a telltale pink bakery box, with maybe one or two remaining frosted donuts. When an outsider comes in bearing a precious gift like that for the office, they vanish almost instantly. Years, ago, before the falling knives that were my health issues, my assistants knew to keep a watchful eye, and they would make sure to set aside a rainbow sprinkle donut, my very favorite, before they all disappeared.

I told myself that the donut was a delightful reward that I deserved, a miniature trophy, a gifted rainbow amidst the clouds. I told myself it was a reward not just for getting through that crazy-busy midday, but also for the previous seven years of nine- to ten-hour days and my working every

Saturday morning; all my efforts were finally showing signs of paying off. Exhausted but proud, I was ready to reap the rewards.

I also wanted to reward myself for holding my chaotic personal life together too, even if by a weak thread. As a new mom, I was mostly on my own during the week as my then-husband, adrenaline-filled with his own success, traveled worldwide for his work.

Daily, I lovingly dressed and diapered the girls for daycare, prepared their organic snacks and day totes, made a mental note of what groceries to get later, quickly breast-pumped before I pulled my business suit on, mailed the house bills, drove to the drop-off area, and kissed the girls goodbye. Exhausted by 8:30 A.M., I couldn't muster even a shred of care for myself. Can you relate?

Back then, other than rewarding myself with a sprinkle donut, I ate for only two reasons: to satisfy my hunger and to give me enough energy to get by. Therefore, the convenience of my food was paramount. To say that my diet was my last priority and furthest thing from my mind was indeed true.

For lunch at work, I savored a bag of convenient Cheetos. I only had so much time at the office, I was *doing* so well at my career, and I felt I had to maximize my efficiency.

My easy go-to solo dinner was a rice flour pizza crust that I would smear with pesto sauce, my only greens for the day. I used to tell myself that pesto was *sort of* a vegetable.

A favorite dinner with my husband, when we finally had some alone time together on Friday nights, was takeout from our favorite neighborhood Italian restaurant in San Francisco; we ordered a rich penne and pancetta pasta with a creamy red sauce, with hardly a vegetable to be seen. I remember being aware that it wasn't the healthiest choice, but our Herculean efforts that week to *do well* surely deserved some serious comfort food. We would gobble it straight out of the takeout containers, exhausted.

It makes me cringe to tell you, but I repeated this nutrient-empty daily eating pattern for more than four *years*. Given the low nutrition fuel I was putting into my body, I shouldn't have been surprised that I eventually attracted three very serious, chronic illnesses. Looking back, I see that of all the universal spokes on my Well-Being Wheel, this seemed to be the most truly off-kilter one.

I have seen a version of this unhealthy eating pattern in dozens of other high-achieving souls. In fact, one of the reasons I wasn't alarmed about my diet back then was that everyone around me ate similarly. I told myself that my crap diet was temporary and that something had to give until I got over the success hump I was striving for at work. The issue is that, for many, this someday turns into years. Have you seen this too?

In our workforces, we are juggling so many personal and professional balls at once that often we eat what is *convenient*, not what is most energizing. Our culture has willingly stepped up to the crisis, and thus we have coffee shops, convenience stores, and drive-throughs on every corner. No wonder we have an entire workforce culture powered by a grab-and-go diet.

Is there another option? You bet there is.

THE RISE OF THE UNIVERSAL *EAT A HEALTHY, PLANT-CENTRIC DIET* SPOKE

One thing that a great education will teach you is how to research things, and gratefully, mine sure did. Since food is our body's main fuel, since it has an undeniable impact on health, and since, in my opinion, it is one of the easiest things to change (not to mention my bad diet had nowhere to go but up), I made the executive decision that my well-being revamp would start with my food.

Like any keen business person embarking on a long-term project, I looked for *success patterns*. What were the country's leading nutritionists and the most highly reputed, top integrative medicine doctors saying about nutrition, disease eradication, and its connection to vibrant well-being? I did not have time to waste. I was so desperately sick, and I needed to make positive progress as fast as humanly possible. Was there any similar agreement in the nutrition research? The answer was yes, yes, and yes. I learned that food is a critical part of healing and a critical part of staying well.

Because I had so much inflammation in my body, Dr. Andrew Weil's groundbreaking anti-inflammatory diet recommendations formed the key foundation of my new eating protocol. As a world-renowned leader and pioneer in the field of integrative medicine, Dr. Weil offers a medical approach that embodies body, mind, and spirit well-being. There are more than 10 million copies of his books sold, and his commonsense approach resonated well with me.

Contrary to what many of us learned with our carbohydrate-laden food pyramids in grade school, at the very foundation of Dr. Weil's Anti-Inflammatory Food Pyramid suggestions are a recommended *minimum* of four or five servings a day of vegetables, raw and cooked, from all parts of the color spectrum.[2] Just this one foundational shift was a tsunami of change for me! I went from eating no veggies (seriously) to eating *mostly* veggies.

To get in those vegetables, I began by going hard-core (yes, admittedly, I can be intense) and focused on getting more greens. I replaced my morning pastry with a green smoothie drink that I still blend in my Vitamix daily:

1 organic cucumber, sliced into 1-inch pieces
1 small avocado, pitted, peeled, and halved
1 cup of organic spinach leaves
1 lime, peeled
1 tablespoon organic flaxseeds or hempseeds
4 ounces water

I don't need to tell you that this green smoothie tastes *nothing* like a rainbow sprinkle donut! With absolutely no sweetness, it wasn't easy to get down at first. However, I made myself do it. In fact, desperate for a change in my health situation but still loving convenience, I often made extras of this green concoction and brought another tumbler of it to work for lunch.

Dr. Weil's suggestions also inspired me to add several servings a day of fruits,[3] and I selected some low-glycemic choices: raspberries and blueberries. I began eating gluten-free oats and brown rice. I took a good look at Dr. Weil's insight on healthy fats,[4] which are rich in omega-3s; I found that it was easy to grab a small handful of walnuts as a snack to replace my Cheetos.

I also relied on the work of Dr. Joel Fuhrman, MD, President of the Nutritional Research Foundation. Dr. Fuhrman is a six-time *New York Times* bestselling author with a focus on, you guessed it, nutritional research. After reading his book *Super Immunity: The Essential Nutrition Guide for Boosting Your Body's Defenses to Live Longer, Stronger, and Disease Free,* I was inspired to add a layer of critical refinement to my diet, with an emphasis on carefully chosen superfoods to boost my immune system not only to reverse disease but also to remain disease-free.

Dr. Fuhrman's "Top Superfoods for Super Immunity" are kale/collards/mustard greens; arugula/watercress; green lettuce and cabbage; broccoli and Brussels sprouts; carrots and tomatoes; onions and garlic; mushrooms; pomegranates; berries (all types); and seeds (flax, chia, sesame, and sunflower).[5] I noted how simple this list was and appreciated the overlap with Dr. Weil's work. Basically, if I was on an island, had fewer than 20 foods to choose from forever, and wanted to be maximally healthy, these would be them.

Dr. Fuhrman's work also convinced me to choose more plant-based rather than animal-based protein, which was a giant shift for me in a healthful direction. He firmly believes that eating plant protein is superior to eating animal protein; he asserts that plant foods not only deliver protein but also "supply you with a host of antioxidants to protect."[6]

Lastly, Dr. Leigh Erin Connealy's research, as described in her book *The Cancer Revolution: A Groundbreaking Program to Reverse and Prevent Cancer,* provided me with even more customized, powerful advice for an alkaline-focused, disease-preventing, detoxifying, correctly supplemented diet plan. Dr. Connealy, who has been practicing medicine for more than 30 years and is the medical director for her integrative medical centers in Irvine, California, believes "most people are allergic to what I call the 'sensitive seven' and have an inflammatory response to many or all of the following foods, so pay particular attention to how you feel after eating these foods. Or you could simply eliminate them from your diet." The foods on her list of concerns include dairy products, wheat, sugar, corn, soy, eggs (eggs are often okay if they are organic), and peanuts.[7] I cut the first three out of my diet for good, which was just right for *my* particular body, adding another healthy overlay to my diet.

As someone with zero nutrition background, I found the research and suggestions of Dr. Weil, Dr. Fuhrman, and Dr. Connealy to be efficient and sensible, and they ignited me in an overwhelmingly positive way, giving me a directional launchpad. My diet went from processed foods to whole foods, from artificially colored to naturally vibrant, and from insubstantial to nutritious. This single spoke was a total game-changer.

THE *EAT A HEALTHY, PLANT-CENTRIC DIET* SPOKE AND WEALTH-BEING

What did vastly improving my *Eat a Healthy, Plant-Centric Diet* spoke do for me? By giving my body the nutrition and high-quality fuel it was craving, it launched me on my way *toward* this spoke's positive personal outcome on the Wealth-Being Wheel: perfect health. I only saw *a glimmer* of this at first, but my body started to run better. Within two weeks, people at work took notice. One of my managers said I looked more "alive" and asked me what I was doing. The truth? Finally getting nutrition!

My inflammation lowered substantially in the first six months, and my hands and feet felt about a third less painful. Before I discovered this spoke, I could not jog for the life of me; the pain was so excruciating in my feet and knees that I had even considered getting a handicapped placard for my car. Six months in, however, I miraculously ran our local 5k for the Fourth of July—not entirely pain-free and moving as slow as a turtle, but, nonetheless, running. I have a photo of me crossing the finish line with my arms in the air.

As far as positive professional outcomes, thought leadership on the Wealth-Being Wheel speaks to how I can think more sharply and more strategically at work. My career requires intensely clear thinking, and I imagine your career does too; there's a lot at stake. With my green smoothie in the car on my way to work, I am already fueled up with dense nutrition—brain food—by the time I step into my downtown office.

Since I am no longer starving or fighting low blood sugar from skipping lunch, I now have a much more commanding presence and skilled communication mastery. When meeting with clients, I am able to focus on them; my body feels calm and grounded. I used to have trouble with eye contact, but now I am able to connect and be in the moment. With no distractions, it's easy for me to access the perfect advice for them, delivered in the exact right, helpful tone; this has made closing business infinitely easier.

Are you ready to experience this game-changing spoke? Let's go.

CUSTOMIZING THE *EAT A HEALTHY, PLANT-CENTRIC DIET* SPOKE FOR YOU

1. Part of taking control of your eating is knowing exactly what you eat now and being brutally honest with yourself about it. Write down everything you typically eat. Note the amount of processed foods. How much color is there? How many veggies? Make a list. When you identify anything unhealthy, cross it out.
2. Look through the categories of Dr. Weil's Anti-Inflammatory Pyramid on his website,[8] noting his food recommendations and the ones that seem to resonate with you in each of his recommended categories. For instance, for fruit, you might choose blueberries, if it's a favorite of yours. That would be a great customization for you.

3. Note if any of your current diet choices are reflected in Dr. Fuhrman's Top Superfoods for Super Immunity list (provided earlier in this chapter). Yes? Good for you! Keep those and consider eating more of them. Do you see any food choices on Dr. Fuhrman's list that you could consider *adding* to your diet? Do you like broccoli but you don't usually eat it? That would be another ideal customization for you.

4. Try Dr. Connealy's advice on testing whether some or all of her "sensitive seven" affect you negatively. There is wide consensus these days that white sugar is unhealthy. Cutting back or cutting it out altogether might be a good improvement.

5. This may sound like strange advice at first, but try using a layer of *intuition*—your deep inner knowing. As I mentioned the different recommendations in the work of Dr. Weil, Dr. Fuhrman, and Dr. Connealy, what stood out to you? We often intuitively know what our body needs, but we don't tap in to hear the wisdom. Add something intuitively chosen to your customized list.

6. Combining your new recommendations, update your new baseline food plan, or at least your list of target foods. It's that easy. This is your new shopping list. Put it somewhere handy, like in your phone.

7. Inspired? Seek out books by Dr. Weil, Dr. Fuhrman, and Dr. Connealy. All of these books are incredibly insightful for those who want to dig deeper.

8. Do your own exploration. There are dozens and dozens of books out on the ketogenic diet, the low-carb anti-cancer diet, and so forth. See what resonates for your specific constitution.

9. Feeling unsteady in this area of diet? Hire a qualified, registered dietician or licensed nutritionist to help you customize a plan that is just right for you.

INCREDIBLE WELL-BEING CUSTOMIZATIONS FROM AN EXCEPTIONAL EXECUTIVE

John Mackey, Cofounder and CEO, Whole Foods Market

During a typical weekend, John Mackey and his wife, Deborah, do some batch cooking, using a pressure cooker to cook black beans (which he soaks overnight), along with a variety of vegetables such as sweet potatoes, carrots, onions, bok choy, broccoli, green beans, asparagus, and kombu (seaweed). He and Deborah eat this stew as a bowl and use it as a filling for burritos, using whole-grain tortillas with added avocado, cilantro, tomatoes, salsa, and a bit of nutritional yeast. John points out that it not only is healthy but also only takes him about 30 minutes start to finish, and that they get three to four meals out of it.

They also love their new countertop steam oven, a recent upgrade to their diet and food prep, because they easily make massive plates of steamed vegetables for dinner. He uses his Vitamix to make one of the easy and delicious no-oil dressings from his book, usually using avocado, nuts, or seeds for a little healthy fat.

There may not be a better executive on the planet to inspire us with this *Eat a Healthy, Plant-Centric Diet* spoke than John Mackey. Because of his expansive knowledge on this topic, his conscious commitment, and his carefully thought-out food strategies, he implements this spoke with a jaw-dropping level of mastery. How does he show up with such power? For one, by means of his food choices.

Recognized as *Fortune*'s "World's 50 Greatest Leaders," Ernst & Young's "National Entrepreneur of the Year," *Barron*'s "World's Best CEO," and *Esquire*'s "Most Inspiring CEO," John has a legendary level of vision and career success. Capitalized with only $45,000 in the late 1970s, he and his partner opened his first natural food store in Austin, Texas. In the years since, Whole Foods Market has grown to nearly 500 stores and has become synonymous with vibrant, organic, healthy eating and conscious community engagement. In 2017, when

Amazon bought Whole Foods for just under $14 billion, John remained the CEO.

Because John is so personally committed to what he terms a "whole foods diet," and so passionate about empowering others to reach their highest health potential, he coauthored *The Whole Foods Diet: The Lifesaving Plan for Health and Longevity.*[9] As he puts it, "You teach what you want to learn." This book is a masterful summary of a huge body of medical science proving that a whole foods, plant-based diet is optimal. John mentions that he likes the easy phrase "Nothing bad added, nothing good taken away," from his friend Michael Greger, MD.

John has a casual manner, clear blue eyes, and an incredible presence. He is thoughtful and precise. He says the main key to success for this *Eat a Healthy, Plant-Centric Diet* spoke is to think and plan ahead.

For breakfast, he capitalizes on the fact that fruits and vegetables "are by far the healthiest foods," and he starts with berries—maybe blueberries, blackberries, or raspberries—and perhaps something in season, like a sumo orange. He adds that he often makes steel-cut oats, one of his very favorite foods, which he says he "could eat for breakfast, lunch, and dinner."

Lunch is healthy, fast, and efficient too. His office, on the top floor of the Whole Foods Market headquarters in Austin, is conveniently above the massive flagship store, so for lunch, he simply walks downstairs for an oil-free stir-fry, a sweet potato, or a salad.

What about the many business dinners John attends? Again, his secret to success is to think and plan ahead. He says, "For instance, if I have a business dinner in Seattle scheduled for the next day, I'll have my assistant call the restaurant in advance to ask the chef to prepare me a vegan, whole foods, no-oil dinner." He humbly admits that he's in a great situation, because normally the chef knows who he is and is honored to make something special for him. But, John says, if the chef doesn't want to do anything special, he will preorder a baked potato or just a plate of steamed vegetables. He points out that any of us could do this: call a restaurant in advance and ask for a healthy dinner.

If he finds himself in a business situation where he may not get any healthy food, like at a catered dinner, he eats before he goes, or he just doesn't eat. He makes a good point: "If you watch other people eat, they are focused on their own food, and not paying attention to you; the food-eating part of these dinners lasts for all of fifteen minutes usually. You are there for the conversation anyway." He makes others feel comfortable if they ask why he's not eating by saying, "You know, I had a big lunch" or "I am just not hungry right now."

How does he master this spoke with his near-constant travel? John always brings his own food on airplanes, usually packing blueberries and nuts. He notes that even if he upgrades, which he does frequently, most airlines don't have healthy or vegan options, so he comes prepared. John doesn't waste time in airport food court lines, and he's snacking on something that boosts his energy.

For John, having those steel-cuts oats for breakfast is not just energy-boosting; it is also personally grounding, no matter where he is. In fact, if he plans to be on one of his many business trips for more than three days, he actually *packs a rice cooker* into a checked bag so he can make breakfast in his room. He explains, "I like the ritual of being on the road, and before I go to sleep, putting my steel-cut oats into the rice cooker to soak overnight. I just punch the button when I get up, and about twenty minutes later, I have a super-healthy breakfast for pennies." As for efficiency, he adds, "It is fast. It simplifies breakfast. And, in a pinch, it takes care of dinner. How easy is that? I don't waste time." This is a perfect example of how John, like other Exceptional Executives, consciously amasses power in his free time. For him, everything he does matters.

Smiling, energized, and looking about 10 years younger than he is, John explains that over time, "Your body gets used to eating a really super-healthy diet. Your palate evolves."

In mastering the *Eat a Healthy, Plant-Centric Diet* spoke, John shows how optimal nutrition can fit seamlessly into any executive or entrepreneur's lifestyle, *especially* if you are crazy-busy. He proves that it doesn't have to be time-consuming (his strategies save time) or expensive (making your own healthy food or bringing your own food on the plane saves money). Most important, he demonstrates perfectly what it looks like to fuel yourself to perform at your highest potential, with the most nourishing foods, completely customized for peak performance during meeting-packed days. No wonder he's the CEO.

John says he feels his best with these plant-based whole foods, with his diet being his top well-being strategy, and he believes that this approach would have similar, positive effects for others too. He concludes that "the body, mind, and spirit all want to be healthy," and that if we align our lifestyle patterns with the right nutrition, we can see that inevitable standout success sooner rather than later.

Get Enough Sleep: It's Not Just the Room Temperature

"A good laugh and a long sleep are the two best cures."[1]
—Irish Proverb

A CAVING MATTRESS

There I was, lying on my back in bed, trying not to move too much as I got settled in. I slowly tucked the sheet in near my neck and plumped the pillow under my knees. I straightened my back ever so slightly and then lay completely still.

You see, with my particular version of chronic pain, if I moved even an inch, I felt a sharp, nail-like jab in the part of me that moved—either my hands, elbows, feet, or knees. Back then, with the alarm-like quality of the pain, I woke up every two or three hours, every night. I knew this was crushing my well-being by increasing my exhaustion, inflating my frustration, and adding to my sense of falling-knife futility, but what to do?

As I tried to relax, I felt the gentle dip in the middle of our mattress. My right hand sunk lower than my left, as the mattress caved in toward the center. Every night, my then-husband and I eventually ended up side by side in that cratered middle. He seemed totally cozy ("I love this bed!"), but I was overheated and uncomfortable. Back then, in our mid-thirties, we agreed that saving as much as we could trumped buying an expensive new bed, and I was too exhausted to even discuss this potential remedy anyway.

I was easily woken by even the slightest sound, and I felt like I was on high alert for our family. My husband slept so deeply, I knew that he wouldn't hear the girls if they cried, so I developed a belief that I needed to be ready. Our toddler often woke up fussing in the middle of the night, and on those occasions I slowly headed to her room, limping in pain, to get her some warm milk or gently rub her back.

And then there I was again, back in bed, carefully tucking the sheet up to my neck again and plumping the pillows. By that point, however, I also struggled with tearful anger about my incessant pain, frustration that I heard every sound, worry about my toddler, and, because of the irrefutable contrast, a growing resentment for the blissfully sleeping man next to me. There he was, night after night, gently snoring, able to sleep for a solid seven or eight hours without a single interruption, his body beautifully reviving for the busy day tomorrow. In contrast, I spent countless hours wide awake, simultaneously experiencing both marvel and annoyance.

My suffering body craved sleep so much that I frequently nodded off in the passenger seat as my husband drove our family to the petting zoo and the park. On weekends, I stumbled into our bedroom for two-hour afternoon naps after the kids went down for theirs. One day at work, I was so crushingly tired that I honestly thought about crawling under my gigantic desk for a 30 minute snooze. I was becoming more and more zombie-like, and sicker with every passing month.

I learned that deep exhaustion can zap you of creativity and your sense of humor. Has that ever happened to you? When my body craved sleep so much that I stopped being funny, I knew something had to change.

THE RISE OF THE UNIVERSAL *GET ENOUGH SLEEP* SPOKE

When I started to research the importance of getting enough sleep and its profound effect on well-being, I learned that there are many people like me who, for a myriad of legitimate reasons, struggled to get enough sleep. On the other hand, there were others who knowingly sacrificed it, intentionally staying up to work on that proposal due tomorrow or binge-watching their favorite series. Regardless, I quickly confirmed that a pervasive lack of sleep hurts your ability to think and function, and it can easily crush your well-being and success.

In our modern culture, we don't honor the immensely positive power of sleep enough. I certainly didn't. I felt like sleep was one of my weaknesses, something that I wished I didn't need, something that was evasive and difficult to achieve, something that I wasn't "good at." Fortunately, once I began to think about treating my sleep challenges with the care they deserved—and started to treat sleep itself with respect—my well-being took a giant leap for the better.

Because this is such a pervasive and elusive well-being issue, there are entire books and dozens of websites on the subject of getting a better night's sleep. In the spirit of our executive summary-style approach, let's touch on some of the most impactful solutions that worked for me.

First, the blissful result of investing in a new mattress shocked me. No longer drifting to the middle, I bow to today's incredible technology. In my opinion, it's worth every dime.

Second, I took hold of my racing mind. In the camp of the people who struggle to get enough sleep, many high-functioning executives and entrepreneurs complain that their mind is so active before bedtime or even in the middle of the night, brimming with thoughts of what happened and what's next, even though they are physically tired, they can't calm down enough to fall asleep. James Findley, PhD, Clinical Director of the Behavioral Sleep Medicine Program at the University of Pennsylvania Perelman School of Medicine, acknowledges, "Worries keep people awake, and they don't have to be negative worries. It could also be something positive you're planning, like a trip or a big event with a lot of things you have to remember."[2] He and many others recommend that before you go to bed, you should physically write everything down—as detailed as possible—on a list. This can really help clear your mind. I started to do it in the evenings with great success.

I also have a *mental* version of this suggestion, which I started using nightly. First, I imagine a garbage can beneath my body. Then, energetically, I release all my cares and worries into it. It's like a giant sigh of relief, and it works quite well too. Its power lies in your intention to move that scattered, nervous energy out of your body, signaling to your internal systems that it's time to embrace some well-deserved rest.

Third, with my sleep improving, I gave some thought to how much sleep is ideal for me, what amount helps me feel like my personal best. I came up with a whopping nine hours a night. (If that sounds like a lot, keep in mind that I was chronically ill at the time.) I couldn't change my morning wakeup time, so I decided to start going to bed earlier.

On that note, many people haven't a clue how much sleep is ideal for their specific body. The National Heart, Lung, and Blood Institute, a Division of the US Department of Health and Human Services, generally recommends that for adults over 18, seven to eight hours a night is ideal.[3] The institute also points out the frightening concept of "sleep debt,"[4] which is *the accumulation of sleep loss* that adds up over time. They note that if you lose two hours of sleep a night, your weekly sleep debt is 14 hours. You know as well as I do how impossible it is to make up those 14 hours, so the disaster to our well-being easily compounds. Avoid sleep debt as much as possible.

Fourth, I stopped drinking coffee in the late afternoon. Everyone is different here—I have met executives who drink coffee after dinner with no issues—but generally, caffeine in our system jacks us up, and this is an easy fix.

Fifth, I also experimented by cutting out wine in the evening. The very next night, I started to sleep more soundly, and I stopped waking up so often. I have had many executives and entrepreneurs share similar experiences after they ditched the nightly nightcap. You think it's helping you relax, but there's an issue with it.

Charlene Gamaldo, MD, an associate professor of neurology, pulmonary, and critical medicine and the director of the Neuro-Sleep Division at John Hopkins Hospital, explains, "Alcohol is a depressant, which can help somebody feel like it's relaxing them and helping them to fall asleep, but alcohol also is rapidly metabolized in your system and, when your body washes the alcohol out, it's more likely to cause what we call a rebound alertness."[5] No wonder!

Finally, over the years, I have refined my sleep environment further, truly elevating my master bedroom to a deeply restful sanctuary. I removed all the previous clutter, so today, there isn't a single piece of clothing on the floor or anything out of place. I added velvet-backed blackout curtains and some low-key decorative lights, which give off a beautiful, restful glow; bought some artistic, uplifting spiritual images to hang above my bed; upgraded the sheets; and added luxurious faux fur blankets. Honestly, now, I can't wait to crawl in.

THE *GET ENOUGH SLEEP* SPOKE AND WEALTH-BEING

What did the complete reinvention of my *Get Enough Sleep* spoke do for me? It had the effect of self-delivering something akin to much-needed CPR. As far as positive personal outcomes, I finally experienced rejuvenation, something that I had doubted I would ever experience again. It felt as if I was coming out of an intense fog. Improvement in this spoke seems exponentially important for well-being; the more sleep I got, the better I felt, the more my pain subsided, and the happier I became. Did it make all my pain subside? No. But did it improve? Yes.

There is just no comparison between me fully rested and me exhausted. Rested, I am funnier, more patient, more thoughtful to family and friends, and more present.

As far as positive professional outcomes on the Wealth-Being Wheel, my *Get Enough Sleep* spoke immediately improved my brain function, and while at work, I noticed I could think more quickly, make decisions more decisively, and react with more groundedness.

Gone were the days where I fantasized about sleeping under my desk. Instead, I would finish a project with (dare I say) a flourish, and move over the paperwork for the new one. I stopped sighing with exhaustion. I stopped groaning when issues would arise (and you know they do). For me, this directly pointed to maximum profitability and, eventually, led to increased financial freedom.

Arianna Huffington, a formerly sleep-deprived business power-house, did extensive research with doctors and scientists for her 2010 TEDWomen talk. She told the audience, "I am here to tell you, the way to a more productive, more inspired, more joyful life is to get enough sleep."[6] I could not agree more.

CUSTOMIZING THE *GET ENOUGH SLEEP* SPOKE FOR YOU

1. Let's start with your current reality. How well do you sleep at night? How alert are you during the day? Rank yourself between totally exhausted and superbly rested. Could you benefit from some improvement?
2. Make a list of what is preventing you from having a great night's sleep. Write down everything you can think of, and one by one, consider how you might solve each. Some (like a bad mattress) are easier to solve than others (like a baby who wakes). Work on what you can change first.
3. Does noise wake you up? That's a pervasive one. Would wearing earplugs be an option? How about a white noise sound machine?
4. Does your mind race before bed? If the previous suggestions for a written list or mental garbage can aren't enough, try the Calm

App or something similar, which allows you to select bedtime stories specifically designed to drone you to sleep. Alternately, you can use apps like this one to choose customized background noises, such as softly lapping water.

5. What's the state of your sleep area? Is it set up for a beautiful, calm rest? Think of ways to sweep away any energy of chaos from the area.

6. Do you have an undiagnosed sleep disorder? Many people don't even know they suffer from sleep apnea. I learned this first-hand when I had to share a hotel room with a relative who wakes up every few minutes but didn't even realize it. Sleep disorders take a huge toll on your body after awhile. Get this checked out by a medical professional if you think this may be an issue for you.

7. For those wanting even more extensive solutions, I recommend Arianna Huffington's book *The Sleep Revolution*, as well as her Sleep Resources website,[7] which offers extensive, well-thought-out suggestions for busy people like us.

INCREDIBLE WELL-BEING CUSTOMIZATIONS FROM AN EXCEPTIONAL EXECUTIVE

Denise Brosseau, Founder and CEO, Thought Leadership Lab

When Denise Brosseau was 18 months away from a milestone birthday, she decided to spend the next year in deep overhaul mode, intent on getting herself in the best shape of her life by jumping in with two feet.

After receiving inspiration from a successful friend and undertaking some careful research, Denise was further motivated by her elderly mother's increasing struggle to get around. Denise says, "When I am that age [eighties], I want to be spry. I want to be driving. I still want to be traveling."

She had also been experiencing a brewing perfect storm of creeping weight gain, menopause brain fog, a diagnosed thyroid issue, and—perhaps most significantly—maddening nighttime insomnia. She explains, "I had a real lack of energy, not wanting to get up off the couch. That's not a good thing. It was time to switch things up."

Denise is a "get it done" person of deep thoughtfulness and significant accomplishment. As the CEO and founder of Thought Leadership Lab, she is an expert on the process of helping leaders build trust, credibility, followers, influence, and strategic connections so that their ideas have maximum reach and impact. As the preeminent Thought Leader on Thought Leadership (a phrase that makes people laugh when she's introduced), she authored *Ready to Be a Thought Leader? How to Increase Your Influence, Impact, and Success*,[8] and it remains the cornerstone book on the topic. Her LinkedIn Learning course on the subject[9] garnered 125,000 downloads within just a few months of being launched.

Before that, Denise, who is a Wellesley graduate with a Stanford MBA, cofounded the Forum for Women Entrepreneurs (FWE), now known as Watermark, which she nurtured and then grew for 10 years into the country's leading organization for women-led startups. Also, she cofounded Springboard, a women's startup launch pad, which offered the first venture capital conference for women entrepreneurs and which has resulted in more than $7 billion in funding to women-founded and women-led businesses. In 2014, the *Silicon Valley Business Journal* honored her as one of the Top 100 Women of Influence, and she was recognized by the Obama White House as a Champion of Change.

On any given day, Denise may be working one on one with a high-level leader or with one of her many business clients, such as the David and Lucille Packard Foundation, the California Community College Chancellor's Office, Planned Parenthood, or eBay. Consequently, her shocking well-being slump, which had her gravitating toward the couch rather than out changing the world, needed a fast turnaround. She embraced a scientifically grounded eating program called Bright Line Eating, based on the *New York Times* bestselling book by the same title,[10] and she noticed an immediate benefit from eliminating flour, sugar, and caffeine from her diet. She went on to lose more than 60 pounds over the next 12 months.

Simultaneously, sensing that her sleep issues held the key to imminently better wellness, she tackled them with care and thoughtfulness. Although she had slept well all her life, over the previous seven years she had gradually experienced what she described as "a complete wipeout" of her ability to sleep through the night.

Determined to get to the bottom of these issues, she began by identifying her sleep challenges and studying them with care. She notes, "I soon discovered that there were three different patterns. Pattern 1 was to go to sleep, wake up three or four hours later, be up for two or three hours, and then finally fall asleep again. Pattern 2 was to go to sleep, wake up five hours later, and be up for the rest of the night. Pattern 3 was being wide awake because of sugar or caffeine until about 1:00 A.M. and then falling asleep but not having enough time to get a good rest before morning." To make matters worse, each night was a mystery waiting to happen; she never knew which of the three patterns she'd experience.

As she began to eliminate sugar, flour and caffeine, she realized just how sensitive her body is, and this greatly informed her sleep-remodeling project. Even the smallest amounts of sugar, like in her favorite barbecue sauce, could push her right back into a sleepless or restless night.

In addition, she explains, "I have a *really* low pain threshold. When I go to the dentist, they need to give me two or three shots of Novocain before filling a cavity while others might be fine with just one. At the hair stylist, brushing my hair too hard causes an immediate pain sensation. To me, everything hurts more."

Fortunately, she noticed that her successful weight loss provided welcome pain relief and better sleeping. She says, "When you are a speaker like I am and doing full-day workshops and standing for hours, when aches and pains can happen to anyone, it gets exacerbated with extra pounds. At the end of that kind of busy day, getting comfortable enough to sleep is *much* less challenging when you are at a healthy weight."

On the subject of comfort, Denise says that one of her most valued purchases is her Sleep Number brand bed, which allows her to make instant adjustments to her mattress firmness. She also remembers, "I tried about five different pillows before I found one that I love, and I take it with me everywhere. Yes, I check a bag, and pack my pillow, even for an overnight trip."

In addition to being sensitive to food and pain, she also noted that she has become increasingly sensitive to noise. When she was younger, she lived on a loud, busy street with no issues, but, she says, "Now, as I get older, every noise triggers me awake."

Because of her commitment to improving her sleep, she explains, "Now I live in a place that is really quiet. My house is completely silent, and I am very intentional about that. I have no ticking clocks, for example. That would drive me crazy." She adds, "Before bed, all my technology goes into a little bedside drawer to charge overnight; the drawer literally closes while the lights go out."

Because a good night's sleep is paramount when Denise is traveling for a workshop or speech, she takes no chances: "I bring earplugs on every trip. I have a kind that I really like—bright pink ones—and I have a whole bag of them."

Lastly, she carefully studied the concept of sleep habits and ideal body rhythms. She was particularly inspired by the book *Why We Sleep: Unlocking the Power for Sleep and Dreams*,[11] by Matthew Walker, PhD. She realized that she's most awake and highly functioning in the morning from 6:00 A.M. to 10:00 A.M., and also in the evening from 9:00 P.M. to 1:00 A.M. (she's both an early bird *and* a night owl). Because of the flexibility of running her own company and her senior level of success, she began experimenting by taking naps during her least energetic time between 5:00 P.M. and 8:00 P.M. She describes her newfound schedule as "my perfect world."

Denise reports that "living my real cycle" has been an astonishing game-changer, and this new pattern is ideal for her particular needs.

With this schedule in place, she can power through her day, nap for an hour or so in the early evening, stay up to enjoy her prime wakeful hours until midnight or 1:00 A.M., and then consistently sleep straight through until morning. Her insomnia dissipated. She has her energy back, she's able to take on more projects than ever before, and she describes herself as "perfectly happy."

Denise readily admits that this sleep cycle setup would be more difficult if she weren't the CEO of her own company; our organizations usually don't operate around *when* a worker is optimally functioning. She understands that many don't have that control, but for those who can schedule meetings in different timeframes, it makes sense to target when you are at your best. She too, has adapted to seize an opportunity. Case in point, she lectured from 3:00 P.M. to 6:00 P.M.—not her favorite time of day—at the Stanford Graduate School of Business for her recent graduate course, Communicating for Credibility. What did she do? She pushed herself, delivered, and received incredible feedback.

Her advice for those who are desperate to sleep better? "I invite people to experiment. Try out four or five different pillows. Experiment with a different mattress. Put up some new dark curtains. Experiment with your food and drink. There are so many different tweaks that you can make. Undertake this project as if you believe things will really improve. As if you matter."

Do Enlivening Exercise:
From Net Sports to Nunchucks

"Don't overthink it. Just begin."[1]

—Rich Roll, Ultra-Athlete

THE PERFECT FOREHAND

There's nothing quite like hitting the ball in the sweet spot of your racket: the solid thwack of the connection, your body moving forward in total balance, and the ball speeding right across the net, top-spinning exactly where you intended, right down your opponent's line. Bliss.

I have been captivated by this *Do Enlivening Exercise* spoke since I was six years old, when my father, who had played tennis in college, placed a junior racket in my hands and started teaching me how to play after school. Tennis enlivened me in every way: I loved the quick pace, sliding back and forth across the court. Once things clicked for me, I was on fire. I started beating my dad, who had been so casually confident about his own skills that he volleyed with a cigar in his mouth, and he and my mom could not have been more proud.

By age 10, I spent weeks with my summer tennis coach in California, and although I was more of a semifinalist than a champion, I loved how I felt about myself in relation to tennis: I felt like a unique individual who was really good at something. When each one of my close friends began middle school cheerleading, I felt the distance, and I sank further into belonging to tennis. I began to look ahead, hope, and make plans so that my decent ability in this sport might be able someday to transport me out of our small, rural Illinois town. And I was right: my ability caught the attention of a boarding school in Connecticut and, later, the attention of the recruiting tennis team at Cornell. And so I took my rackets—and every opportunity.

As I mentioned earlier, I was still playing tennis two weeks before I was diagnosed with rheumatoid arthritis, but, as soon as the arthritis pain set in, even supportive wraps on my wrists didn't help, and my tennis playing came to a screeching halt. It would be a crushing *10 years* before I would play tennis again.

My feet swelled so that every step pierced, my shoulders ached so that moving my arms was agony, and very soon, I stopped exercising altogether. I found myself literally caving in, trying to just get by and to walk as little as possible. I felt I had no choice—but little did I know the dire consequences.

THE CREATION OF THE UNIVERSAL *DO ENLIVENING EXERCISE* SPOKE

The benefits of this *Do Enlivening Exercise* spoke are highly documented and universally accepted in our culture. We all know we are *supposed to get exercise*, right? I knew it back then too, and for someone who was an athlete, or at least athletic, I felt guilty from the start for letting exercise slide out of my life. The Mayo Clinic recommends approximately "150 minutes of moderate aerobic activity or 75 minutes of vigorous aerobic activity a week,"[2] but very few of us get even that.

In order to bring enlivening exercise back, I first had to redefine who I was. Clearly no longer a fabulous tennis player, I reluctantly accepted that, and then I began to rebuild a new image for myself. I was inspired by some research that pointed out four encouraging realities.

First, I learned that **physical exercise boosts energy.** I know this may seem obvious to you, but when I was in chronic pain, I believed that trying to *conserve* energy would *preserve* my energy, akin to hoarding it for safekeeping. This was dead wrong. I started to feel more and more helplessly fatigued as I did less exercise.

Have you ever heard anyone at work, facing a midafternoon slump, say, "I am so tired I either need a nap or a jog?" That's because exercise *enlivens* you. It gives you a second wind!

Second, I assumed that *not* moving my joints would protect them, but without much use, my joints stiffened; my elbow locked at an angle, keeping my arm bent for weeks. The truth is that **physical exercise keeps your body more flexible.**

My physical therapist at the time pointed me to a considerable amount of research from the Arthritis Foundation suggesting that moving and stretching is crucial at helping ease pain and increase flexibility where stiffness is setting in. The overarching advice from the foundation is that "exercise is crucial."[3] This is very hard to believe when it hurts to move, but they are right.

The horrible consequences of a sedentary life are very well-documented and point to higher rates of cancer, heart disease, obesity, dementia, poor skin tone—really, everything we *don't* want. Genetic metabolic neurologist Dr. Mark Tarnopolsky realized that most people are motivated by the positive outcomes of exercise, so he and some colleagues completed a fascinating study in 2011 and found scientific evidence of a host of exercise benefits, like better mood, reduced pain, slowed aging, and better brain function. These benefits were so strong that, as he put it, "It's unbelievable."[4]

In her comprehensive cover article for *Time Magazine*, "The New Science of Exercise," health writer Mandy Oaklander summarizes it perfectly: "If there were a drug that could do for human health every-thing exercise can, it would likely be the most valuable pharmaceutical ever developed."[5] Yes.

Third, I learned that **sweating is more important than you might think.** I wasn't sweating at all during those off years, and as you may know, the function of sweating is not only to cool the body down but also, very importantly, to purge the body of toxins, including heavy metals, bacteria, viruses, excess salt, and excess calcium. When I was recovering from kidney cancer, my oncologist found that I had very high levels of mercury and other metals, so she suggested I use my far infrared sauna a few times a week just to promote more sweating and detoxing.

Fourth, **it's significant that your exercise is enlivening.** If you are committed to exercising, why not have it do double duty by getting you in shape *and* lifting your spirits? If you hate doing the StairMaster, is that resentment running through your body for 30 minutes *really* going to promote well-being for you? Better to pick something you enjoy.

Armed with these four findings, I snapped this spoke back into place in my life with some new customized *Do Enlivening Exercise* choices, which were more in line with my capabilities, and they had an exponen-tially beneficial effect of launching me toward greater well-being.

Yoga got me stretching in ways I never would have tried on my own, not to mention the motivating, community aspect of class, and although I still have to do a plank on my elbows instead of my sensitive hands, I really enjoy it. Walking short distances gave me initial hope. It wasn't as painful as I feared it would be. It also got my blood moving and brought me out into the sunshine.

Jogging followed when the pain in my feet subsided, and although I was running as slow as a turtle, my heartbeat, rising for the first time in three years, felt like it was beating a thump of thanks. Very importantly, it got me sweating again. I jog a few times a week.

Kung Fu has allowed me to take on a new, enlivening, competitive sport with my teen daughters. Since there is no racket holding, I could do this!

We are part of a warm Kung Fu community of kids and adults who are in amazing shape. I am not going to be a black belt anytime soon, but I do advance, and this is really fun and gratifying.

THE *DO ENLIVENING EXERCISE* SPOKE AND WEALTH-BEING

What did reclaiming my *Do Enlivening Exercise* spoke do for me? As far as positive personal outcomes, my stamina increased as I got back into shape. As fresh energy started moving through my body more regularly, I started feeling more…energetic! Funny how that happens!

Also, I felt like more of a participant in my own life, rather than a sad outsider. I joined more family walks and gorgeous hikes at Point Reyes National Seashore. At parents' day for my daughter's horse camp, I participated in the fun and goofy parent-kid ranch games, with my daughter as my happy sidekick.

When I worked out alone, it gave me some newfound "me time" where I was able to get my body back after two births. It was during these reclaimed moments that I knew that exercise in general was good for my soul.

As far as positive professional outcomes on the Wealth-Being Wheel, my *Do Enlivening Exercise* spoke has greatly broadened my overall network. Although I have never approached an exercise opportunity as a prospecting endeavor (and I think most savvy people could see right through that fakeness anyway), I have met many incredible, authentic connections on yoga retreats, at Kung Fu class, on my daily dog walk with my labradoodle, and on my jogging path. These people have bonded with me over a genuine love of the exercise activity at hand. We have something in common—a shared interest—and knowing each other is a win-win for both of us. Although never the original intention, this networking benefit points most clearly to maximum profitability on the Wealth-Being Wheel. It has generated countless referrals.

Are you ready to experience this game-changing spoke? Let's go.

CUSTOMIZING THE *DO ENLIVENING EXERCISE* SPOKE FOR YOU

1. Do you practice any form of regular exercise now? Would you describe it as enlivening in the sense of it lifting your spirits? If yes, let's call that a winning customization for you. Keep doing that! If it is deadening, please reconsider and choose a new exercise option.

2. Before you begin any exercise program, make sure that you have had a doctor's checkup and are cleared to move forward. Assuming you are, decide how much time per day or per week you can commit to. Since the current recommendation is for 150 minutes per week of cardio, aim for close to that. Put the appointments for exercise on your calendar.

3. Think about having an exercise choice for a busy day when you don't have much time and one for a day when you have more time (perhaps on a weekend). Would these be different for you? For example, you might just throw on jogging shoes and do a quick run on a busy day, but go to an hour-long Kung Fu class on Saturday mornings. This way, you don't have an excuse for skipping exercise because of a time crunch.

4. Does your exercise customization make you sweat? Think about adding an exercise intense enough for you to sweat. It's important.

5. Do you think an exercise buddy might help motivate you? Many studies show this helps commitment tremendously. Think of someone who might be an option.

6. Would you be open to watching exercise videos? There are thousands on YouTube, and you can also buy DVDs to use in your home, on everything from cardio to weights.

7. Have you ever thought of doing an exercise retreat? There are countless yoga, surfing, diving, and even nature trail running retreats available. Some people find that the retreat can really jumpstart a lifelong love of that sport.

INCREDIBLE WELL-BEING CUSTOMIZATIONS FROM AN EXCEPTIONAL EXECUTIVE

John Worden, Trial Lawyer, Partner, and Head of San Francisco Litigation Group, Schiff Hardin LLP

After a busy day in court, John Worden usually fits in an hour workout at the gym. He sets the treadmill to the highest incline and holds weights in each of his hands. Headset on, he cranks up his favorite motivating workout music, often a hardcore album by thrash metal band *Megadeth*. He admits that maybe no one else wants to hear it, but says, "I love it in my own little world; it motivates me."

This workout used to take two hours, but he explains that he's cut the time in half by doubling the intensity to make it more efficient. A no-excuses kind of person, John says, "My work hours are long, and so I have to be efficient at the things I do."

After his treadmill, he moves to doing floor work, holding planks for three or four minutes and then completing core exercises on a weight bench, where he puts 35-pound weights in each hand and does crunches that involve pulling his legs up straight, making his body into a V shape. He doesn't do anything halfway. Laughing, he admits that a favorite saying of his is "Nothing in moderation."

John says he swears by "intense workouts" and "competitive events." He explains, "Slow and steady is not going to get me in the shape that I want to be in." He's incredibly focused.

A few days later, on a Saturday afternoon, he's at the martial arts studio in Alamo, California, teaching his popular Double Nunchucks seminar to a packed class of adults and teens. A second-degree black belt in Bok Fu Do, a form of Kung Fu, John, who emits such physical power and personal excellence that it causes a hush of reverence in the room, begins to demonstrate the tournament sequence or form he's teaching everyone. It's a series of 30 to 40 orchestrated moves that shows a person's speed, skill, and control. At the front of the dojo mat, he takes both his nunchucks, and stretching them out in both hands at eye level, he snaps out the slack and instructs, "First, you show your opponent the weapon."

John started in martial arts at age 26, earned his first-degree black belt at 36, and earned his second-degree black belt three years later. When Bok Fu Do students earn their first-degree black belt, they are honored with a carefully chosen spirit animal that represents their essence and characteristics. John's black belt animal is the rhinoceros, and when you consider this animal's massive power, territorial behavior, thick protective skin, and iconic, defensive fighting horn, you see the perfection in the choice.

John has won multiple gold medals at the National Kung Fu Championships, including his light-contact fighter division when he was 50. He used to fight or compete in tournaments every month, and he's won more than 50 trophies, including overall tournament grand champion three times, several gold medals from the National Kung Fu Championships in Baltimore, and a silver medal at the 2003 World Kung Fu Championships in Sao Paolo, Brazil.

He attends some intense workouts with his fellow black belts in the Bok Fu Do system, where he has somewhat of an elder status, and since there are only about 18 of them at this high level of achievement, it's a close group. Although he doesn't do full-contact fighting anymore (the age limit in competition is 35), he does about 12 full-contact practice matches for his fellow black belts every July. Last summer, at age 52, he felt he was in the best shape of his life, and he's committed to working to maintain it.

The following week, he is playing defense (no surprise there) with his indoor soccer team. Played in a walled, indoor area, this version can be even more intense than traditional soccer, as balls can be played off the walls without stopping.

John Worden is a top trial lawyer who has tried dozens of cases, mostly for defendants, in state and federal courts, in front of judges, juries, and binding arbitration panels. In fact, he has won 25 of his last 27 cases. A partner for more than 20 years at Schiff Hardin LLP, a highly reputable mega-firm of 300 lawyers, John helps lead the litigation practice group in San Francisco and heads the firm's Nevada practice. He is one of the youngest elected members of the American Board of Trial Advocates (ABOTA), an invite-only organization comprising the nation's most experienced and respected trial lawyers. Because he enjoys teaching, he's also an adjunct professor at the University of California Hastings School of Law.

John explains that in particular, his martial arts training has helped him become a superior attorney. "The focus is never limited to learning how to fight, but rather on the overall development of the mind, body, and spirit. Although higher-ranking students are unparalleled in their physical development, without exception they have each improved their lives and the lives of those around them in ways seemingly unrelated to the physical arts. As a lawyer who handles high-stakes trials all over the US, I know I need to be able to stand up to almost any challenge. The intense training and extreme pressures I experienced and underwent working toward and receiving my black belt prepared me to withstand the challenges I face in the courtroom."

It takes a very high level of stamina to be at the top of your career game like this. John, who is also a vegan, credits his commitment to exercise, which overall is his top well-being strategy, to his high level of energy. Years and years ago when he wasn't in such good shape, he used to be tired and unproductive after a certain time of day. "Now," he says, "it's easy for me to stay awake."

This stamina fosters his inherent extra-mile attitude, whether it's in the number of weight-lifting reps he does or in his commitment to clients. It supports his overarching, unique generosity of spirit, where he wants to "always help people." He comments, "Successful people are accessible, and I will respond to clients at all hours, day or night, and they know I will solve their problem." For his friends, people he cares about, the martial arts studio, or the community, he's willing to give. For two years in a row, Worden won the San Francisco Bar Association's Volunteer of the Year award for his pro-bono and diversity work.

In November 2018, Worden chose to help someone in a remarkable way: he donated a kidney to someone he's never met. Inspired by his wife, who donated her kidney to save the life of a friend of their daughter, he learned about the process, and because of his extraordinary level of physical fitness, he sailed through the pre-donation physical checkups. He's a bit embarrassed by the publicity within the law community, where the story gained instant momentum. He says, "It really wasn't that tough all things considered, and most things I do, others could do if they tried. They just may not believe (yet) that they can."

John is the perfect Exceptional Executive and role model for the *Do Enlivening Exercise* spoke because he takes exercise to the highest peak. Without a doubt, John is at a professional athlete level. Here's his advice for someone who is just beginning to exercise, who is starting to revive an exercise regiment, or who is trying to get in a few really good workouts a week.

For those who currently do nothing, he echoes ultra-athlete Rich Roll's quote from the start of the chapter and encourages you "to do *something*. You don't need to work out two hours a day. You can get a decent workout in 20 minutes, and even if it is at midnight or four a.m., it can be done."

For someone with just 20 minutes, he recommends his personal favorite, the P90X series,[6] which are "dummied down" so that almost anyone can do them at home. He explains that they come with a booklet with all the exercises, and there's a helpful DVD. There is even a P90X 10-minute workout, which is an absolute upgrade over doing nothing. He suggests that you could do 10 minutes a day and build up.

What about traveling? Since John says he travels "all the time," he has another suggestion: google "Hotel Room Workouts," which identifies at least 20 options ranging from 15 to 20 minutes long. Easy as that.

Finally, John really advocates having a workout buddy, because the peer pressure is truly effective. He mentions that almost every evening, his wife joins him at the gym, and it really helps motivate him to treat it as an appointment that would be unfortunate to break. With his black belt colleagues, his presence provides a formidable sparring partner, which helps secure future national and world wins. With his soccer team, they rely on his ability and the comradery, and he knows that, if he didn't turn up, they would all miss him.

This critical *Do Enlivening Exercise* spoke should inspire you to up-level your well-being—body, mind, spirit—with the tireless determination of the great rhino, galloping with force, unstoppable.

Upgrade Your Products: The Health on the Shelf

"Look into nature, and then you will understand it better."[1]

—Albert Einstein

CRINGE

During the decades before I was stricken with illness, if you had asked my criteria for an excellent deodorant/antiperspirant, my answer would have been twofold: "It totally stops my armpits from sweating and it smells fresh."

If you had asked my standards for overall body lotion, I would have said, "It moisturizes and smells fresh."

As for body wash/soap, I was looking for lots of suds and again, something that smells fresh. I think that you understand I like *fresh*!

I had a thing for body powder back then, too, and before getting dressed, I would puff it all over my torso.

Since my nails were always painted, what essential quality did I require with nail polish? Ideally, it stayed shiny and lasted as long as possible.

For toothpaste? I have always been very conscientious about caring for my teeth and bright smile, but I would have said that any major, recognizable brand would do, as long as it's minty. I couldn't have named a favorite.

As for my skincare, from face serums to eye creams, I did splurge here in terms of spending money, knowing that my extra dollars might attain a product with higher-powered ingredients to reduce signs of aging. Who doesn't want that? My decision here was based on magazine beauty awards, and more important, whether it seemed to smooth the little wrinkles around my eyes and my smile. If it did, I loved it.

As for the cleaning products for our home, my trip down the grocery aisle included grabbing just *whatever*: a toilet bowl cleaner, a glass cleaner, a shower spray, a surface cleaner. I didn't really give this much thought, though I leaned toward products with bleach because I knew bleach kills germs. I also liked pictures of scrubbing bubbles.

Dish detergent was another non-decision, and I chose whatever jewel-toned liquid soap looked inviting. Maybe I'd get that green one, or maybe that yellow one. I absolutely never bought gloves; gloves seemed unnecessary.

I had little knowledge or consideration of the toxic chemicals or unhealthy ingredients or synthetic scents of the products, and yet they were in direct contact with my body, each and every day. A subject I never really considered, product content just didn't seem important or worthy of my attention—until my health got my attention.

THE RISE OF THE UNIVERSAL *UPGRADE YOUR PRODUCTS* SPOKE

As I started doing even the most precursory research, I learned that the *Upgrade Your Products* spoke is a fairly easy way to foster better well-being. And with my complicated health challenges, this spoke seemed like an easy way to upgrade. Initially, I was hoping that I was allergic to something in one of the products I was using, and that stopping it would, like a wand, make my health issues vanish into thin air. That wasn't the case, but what I learned certainly changed my life for the better.

I started my executive-summary-style research by finding highly regarded sources with helpful summaries and noting common ingredients consistently considered potentially unhealthy. There is quite a lot of scientific information out there for anyone wanting to do a deep dive. Here's what I found out.

Sulfates have stirred up a myriad of concerns for consumers, and if you walk down any personal care aisle, and you will see many products, right on the front, advertise NO SULFATES. Why? Sulfate is a chemically derived salt that is a very efficient cleansing and foaming product (think suds and lather) found in things like liquid soaps, shampoos, toothpaste, and laundry detergent. *Sulfate* is an umbrella term for the synthetic sulfate-based chemicals called sodium lauryl sulfate (SLS) and sodium laureth sulfate (SLES). Because these are often produced from petroleum, there are a whole host of environmental issues, but focusing on our health, "SLS and SLES can irritate eyes, skin, and lungs, especially with long-term use. SLES may also be contaminated with a substance called 1,4-dioxane, which is known to cause cancer in laboratory animals. This contamination occurs in the manufacturing process."[2] That substance, 1,4-dioxane, is also known as ether. What surprised me was that "the amount of SLS and SLES in a product depends on the manufacturer. It can range from small amounts to almost 50% of the product."[3]

Parabens are synthetic compounds used since the 1950s to prevent bacteria and to act as a preservative. They can be found in deodorants, lotions, shampoos, conditioners, toothpastes, and other products. On personal care labels, it can be listed as methylparaben, ethylparaben, propylparaben, and several others, all containing that *paraben* part of the word. As noted by the nonprofit Campaign for Safe Cosmetics (CSC), "Of greatest concern is that parabens are known to disrupt hormone function, an effect that is linked to increased risk of breast cancer and reproductive toxicity."[4] In a *Scientific American* article, "Should People Be Concerned about Parabens in Beauty Products?" the authors note,

"Health advocates are pressuring the FDA to ban parabens in products sold in the US—like the European Union did in 2012—but concerned consumers must take matters into their own hands for now by reading product labels and avoiding products with parabens."[5] Self-advocacy is key.

Propylene glycol (PG) is a synthetic liquid alcohol, usually derived from petrochemicals, used as a solvent in perfume, cosmetics, hygiene products, and even in antifreeze, and it acts as a delivery mechanism in topical products. On the nonprofit Environmental Working Group's Skin Deep database (a wonderful resource to search safety ratings of more than 73,000 substances), PG rates as a HIGH concern for irritation (skin, eyes, lungs) and a MODERATE concern for organ system toxicity (nonreproductive).[6] In her article "Propylene Glycol: The Complicated Additive with Potentially Dangerous Side Effects," researcher Rebekah Edwards notes that the chemical is potentially toxic to the kidneys and liver, and probably not safe for infants or pregnant women.[7]

By no means a comprehensive list, this indeed was an actionable place for me to start, and yes, most of my personal care and home-cleaning products contained these chemicals. I changed them all out for better, safer alternatives.

I also learned a lot from a list created by a US-based, direct-to-consumer clean beauty brand, Beautycounter. Beautycounter's "Never List" of 1,500 harmful or questionable ingredients they prohibit from their product formulations, including 1,400 ingredients banned in the European Union,[8] provides a fabulous, alphabetical, one- or two-sentence description of each chemical, and the reason it is questionable. I love an excellent executive summary.

I also found an incredibly helpful resource in the website of cancer survivor and well-being advocate Kris Carr, who uses the Environmental Working Group's safety ratings combined with real-life user reviews for helpful lists of the best natural deodorant,[9] best nontoxic nail polish,[10] and a number of other common products. This saved me time as I swapped out my old selections for new improvements.

I will admit that the hardest change for me for this spoke was switching to a natural deodorant. I was *not* used to my armpits sweating, even when I worked out, because my former antiperspirant, with more than seven powerful synthetic chemicals, including an aluminum-based, active ingredient, did just that!

The Environmental Working Group (EWG) has a helpful list of "Top Green Cleaning Products" on their website, and they include ratings, details on ingredients, and suggestions on dozens of bathroom, dish-washing, floor, kitchen, laundry, and other cleaners.[11] I use this site as a go-to resource for home cleaning. It should also be mentioned that while there are many green brands, another consistently mentioned, effective all-purpose household cleaner is simple white vinegar, which you can get at the grocery store. White vinegar is incredibly cheap, it's natural, and it's tough on bacteria, mildew, and dirt.

Overall, I started to look for plant-based, non-petroleum products with certified organic ingredients. If possible, I also look for the indica-tion of a product being fair trade, which refers to a way of buying and selling products to ensure that producers get fair prices. I think this additional layer helps the energy of products that are making a positive impact across the world.

Admittedly, to switch out so many of your current products can seem daunting. My best advice is to make the change gradually, one product at a time, taking your time to research your choices and upgrade to some-thing you can feel good about. Then that task is done; no need to think about it again. Considering all the money we all spend on self-care prod-ucts and cleaning solutions—how wonderful it feels to be using some-thing that *helps*, not harms!

THE *UPGRADE YOUR PRODUCTS* SPOKE AND WEALTH-BEING

What did vastly improving my *Upgrade Your Products* spoke do for me? This spoke's positive personal outcome on the Wealth-Being Wheel is "glow," or a personal outer radiance. Using natural products seems like a polishing, or a finishing touch, on my outer self. Because I began using natural products on my skin, I found the scents to be more luscious (like the coconut in my lotion) and more lasting.

As far as positive professional outcomes on the Wealth-Being Wheel, my *Upgrade Your Products* spoke is a bit tricky, but I can attest that it brought me more confidence in my behind-the-scenes choices, in my appearance, and in my awareness that I was making an important, conscious step toward more healthful choices. I would have to say the personal confidence it imparted most closely points to peak performance.

Are you ready to tackle this game-changing spoke? This is a straight-forward one to improve on.

CUSTOMIZING THE *UPGRADE YOUR PRODUCTS* SPOKE FOR YOU

1. Make a list or take note of products you currently use on your body and products you use to clean your home. See what we're working with here.
2. If you really are new to this spoke and this type of upgrade, select a product you use and note if any of the three main offenders listed previously—sulfates, parabens, or propylene glycol—are among the ingredients. You can do this with all your care products. If you want to do a more thorough chemical search, you can use the www.beautycounter.com "Never List"[12] or do searches on the Environmental Working Group (EWG) website.[13]
3. Choose one that you could improve on, and try some healthier alternatives on the EWG website, Kris Carr's website,[14] or from your own research. My advice here is to experiment with differ-ent options, as this is a customization for YOU, and our bodies all react differently to lotions, deodorants, and so forth. Also,

we all have different preferences for different natural scents; some of us might love the coconut (me!) while others prefer the citrus scents.

4. Remember that this is a project worth doing, and that once you land on a favorite in one area, you can move to another product to upgrade. Take a moment of gratitude for your work in this area—you are taking a stand for yourself and your well-being. It's so hard to quantify the internal shift a product upgrade will cause, but I believe everything we do matters.

INCREDIBLE WELL-BEING CUSTOMIZATIONS FROM AN EXCEPTIONAL EXECUTIVE

May Lindstrom, Founder, CEO, and Formulator, May Lindstrom Skin

May Lindstrom explains the motivation for her business as follows: "If I could just take a bottle and put a love note in it—like a bottle going down a river—and someone could open that bottle and just love themselves a little more, and that was effective, I would do that. Obviously, I can't just deliver bottles down the river to people, and that note alone wouldn't be powerful enough, so I choose to do a version of this through skin care. That is the idea."

May, who grew up in rural Minnesota, started formulating potions as a child as a way to solve her own chronic skin sensitivities. Her family discovered early on that ingredients in conventional skin care and even so-called natural products gave her blisters, rashes, and eczema. She attained her first hints of relief with pure, single-ingredient solutions she found in her kitchen.

In her twenties, May's passion for formulation evolved into much more serious research into plant medicine. She began sharing bespoke formulations, working one-on-one with clients suffering with extreme skin traumas, from care post-cancer and radiation therapy to severe acne, psoriasis, and dermatitis. She realized that the healing results so evident in this demographic, whom she describes as "in such pain both physically and emotionally," would naturally do wonders on others with complexions in a healthy state. She was right.

In 2011, May Lindstrom Skin, the full-blown, Los Angeles–based skin care brand, was born. This collection up-levels even the green beauty industry's standards on ingredients. May believes that "it's not so much about what we are avoiding (the harsh synthetics and hormone disruptors on all the natural skincare 'No' lists are a given), it's that I think we can do better than that. I am focused on what we are actually putting *in*." She insists on including "the highest possible quality on the planet of each singular ingredient. We are using the freshest, most potent, truly natural plant and mineral ingredients, in their most pure and powerful state."

May sources her fair trade and organic ingredients from around the world, and essentially "from the ground, from the farmer, as untouched and unprocessed as possible to retain all the goodness." She adds, "We take a really beautiful thing and don't mess with it." As an example, she holds up a glass jar of raw, unfiltered avocado oil, one of her prized ingredients. She tips the jar, admires it, and points out that "our avocado oil is so green that it's almost black. It's loaded with chlorophyll, it's filled with nutrition for your skin, it sparkles in the light, and it's simply magic. It's actually beyond magic."

She sources cacao butter in its raw state, "which is rare, but it is so rich, potent, and aromatic, and it retains the exotic fruit's nutrition. It's loaded with antioxidants and incredible for hydration. It's a vital component to our bestselling formula, and it's so good we literally eat it." She says many products we might find on store shelves contain cocoa butter, but "almost always, it is in a bleached, filtered, highly processed form, which is completely different." She adds, "Conventional care products are also typically years old by the time they reach your skin."

May says that her favorite ingredient, blue tansy, a wild African flower in the daisy family, is sourced from Morocco, the only area in the world where it naturally prospers. She explains, "Blue tansy is grown in these really small areas. You can only produce so much, and then the production process is pretty tedious and expensive." It's the star ingredient in her most well-known formulation, The Blue Cocoon, which is a jewel-blue facial melt, significant in that it was one of the first blue tansy products on the market, and because of that, was the product that brought blue tansy to the world's attention. (Endorsements from raving Hollywood fans like wellness advocate Gwyneth Paltrow didn't hurt either.) May says blue tansy "is an incredibly powerful ingredient, great for pain and inflammation. It's also used in aromatherapy for stress and anxiety, and the same thing it does for irritable skin, it also does for the emotions. It touches on both the physical self and the emotional self."

May has spent years securing and nurturing relationships with the farms that grow and harvest blue tansy for her. She says, "It breaks my heart that adulterated versions of 'blue tansy' have popped up prolifically, often cut with chamomile and injected with blue dye to mimic the plant." She says misrepresentation in raw ingredients is rampant in the skin care industry, and consumers passionate about well-being need to make sure they are getting products from reputable brands that will go the extra mile not just in creating clean formulations, but also in ensuring safe and authentic sourcing of the ingredients.

High-quality ingredients are one important aspect of May's company, but she also mentions a key differentiator: "We are built around this idea of *freshness*." Her products are made within days of shipping to a myriad of her website's direct customers. As with eating, freshness delivers higher nutrient content. She explains, "When you eat better, you feel better. When you take care of your skin with real, resonant ingredients, your skin changes too."

Not only are the level of quality ingredients and the freshness aspect impressive, but also May's company values impact. She describes her company as "more than a brand; it's an intimate process." She admits no desire to run a huge factory. Instead, she says, "I aim to be a ripple. So if I raise the bar here and I raise the conversation to not just what we are leaving out but to what we are putting in; how that's sourced from the seed to the soil to the farmer, to the community in which these ingredients are grown, and all the way to our door; how we care for our people; how these products are made in our kitchen with love, care, and intention; how we really celebrate freshness and authenticity; and really just how we are doing 'right' all the way through, then we set an example."

With no outside investors, entirely self-funded through organic sales of the product alone, May can focus on the relationships that matter to her. She has created treasured relationships with each of her employees ("I know their families; I know their children."); her beloved husband, who works alongside her in the company; and with her customers. With every luxury-wrapped order sent out from their studio, May personally handwrites a love note and an affirmation. She says she tries to convey this message: "I see you. You are a human. I want to connect with you. It's really about connection. It's about connection between each other, but it is also about connection back to yourself."

May aims to set an example, via her company, around this idea of intention, of "really creating a catalyst to return to self-care." She says she sees "an opportunity to reignite that romance, and come back to the intentionality of your own touch. Your own hands on your own skin is incredibly powerful, and if we can deliver that twice a day through skin care, that is a totally life-changing thing."

She notes that most of us hustle through our morning and nightly cleansing routines, be it washing our faces, brushing our teeth, or shaving. She says, "We rush through so much that the last thing we need to do is rush through this. These very precious little moments. These are the bookends of our day."

She models her own bookend rituals on her website,[15] even with something as basic as washing her face. Notably, she moves as if in slow motion, with such grace and consciousness. She turns a common practice into something extraordinary.

She also feels that upgrading your products with intentionally made, natural replacements is equally important for both women and men. She does not believe that this is a gender-specific priority, laughing and noting that "we are all human, and we all have skin."

Although May's collection, admittedly, is at a luxury price point, she feels "that it doesn't have to be so inaccessible." She suggests that we can take our chosen self-care products and "make that into a ritual too. The intentionality you bring is up to you." She adds, "We don't need to wait for a completely silent hour, when the kids are in bed and we are finally able to draw a bath and have candles lit to immerse ourselves in a loving ritual or to give care to our skin. If we do that, it's never going to happen. That's just not what life looks like."

As a busy CEO and mom of two young children, May admits she might be doing a facial mask at 9:00 A.M. on a Tuesday while she is doing her first round of emails or any night of the week as she washes the dinner dishes. She says, "I am still giving myself that care. It counts. I count." Her noticeably glowing, immaculate skin gives testimony to the results of this commitment.

To experience May's values is to be invited to return to the basics, to beauty in simplicity, to lush ingredients, and to the transformative power of intentional self-care. A self-described "Mama Bear," she is the warm voice we all need, reminding us that we're worth it.

Hydrate: Hydration Station

"Water is the driving force of all nature."[1]
—Leonardo da Vinci

PARCHED

Before I came down with my illnesses, when I was blissfully ignorant about well-being, I had a very carefully constructed, three-part beverage strategy that I believed gave me the superpowers needed to get through every busy day as a new mom and career woman striving for success. Let me be clear that it was absolutely *not* a hydration strategy, but more of an *energy management* system.

First off, in order to start my day with an enlivening boost, I would drink an extra-large amount of coffee. If I made coffee at home, I would have two or three cups. If I was driving by a favorite coffee shop, I would order their largest-size latte. I knew full well that I was jacking myself up in the morning because I was exhausted, and I couldn't think of anything better than a caffeinated energy boost. Because I also loved the taste, my first sip would be like a reward for waking up. Even the warming heat on my hands made me happy.

I had identified the exact amount of coffee I needed to erase my exhaustion and to feel upbeat, but I was aware that if I crossed the line and had too much, I would become horribly jittery, cranky, and unfocused. Too much coffee caused me to make panicked lists of everything I needed to do, and because I also was cranky, I would get really down on myself. So, back then, I had a coffee limit.

Second, I would drink a bottle of Diet Coke for lunch. I would work diligently at my desk all morning and then feel my energy drop around noon. At that point, even the act of getting up, of figuratively crossing the line into the second half of the day, made this trip to the company break room special. I used to love putting money into the vending machine and hearing the hefty sound of the Diet Coke drop. I loved the bubbles, the taste, and the caffeinated boost that it gave me to jumpstart my afternoon.

Even back then, I was aware that Diet Coke has no nutritional value, so when I was pregnant with my two daughters, to keep them safe, I didn't touch it. After they were born, I went back to it, reticently realizing that I didn't have quite the same care standards for myself.

Third, around dinner time, I would drink two glasses of sauvignon blanc. Even the sound of the cork popping out of the wine bottle signaled that my career work was done for the evening—that it was time to relax and celebrate getting through my day. I loved the crisp taste, and the first sip was like a sigh of relief. I would savor one glass as I made my toddlers their dinner and got them bathed, and then I would enjoy the second when their dad got home from work and we ate our dinner together.

Deep down, I knew that two generous glasses of wine every evening probably wasn't good for me either, but I told myself that it was temporary, that my life wouldn't always be so demanding. I also told myself that we lived just a stone's throw from vintner-laden Napa Valley, and that we certainly weren't the only ones who shared a bottle of wine nightly.

As you can see, I had created a *hoist-me-up* and then *bring-me-down* strategy with my beverages. Although it was intended to be temporary, I did it day after day for more than eight years.

THE RISING TIDE OF THE UNIVERSAL
HYDRATE SPOKE

After I was diagnosed with my first disease, I admitted to my new and promising alternative medicine doctor that I drank no water. None at all. "None?" he asked, as if he'd never heard anyone say that. He was alarmed.

Since I was on a roll with the shock, and desperate for freedom from the pain I was experiencing, I came clean and told him everything. What did I have to lose? I told him I hated the boring taste of water, that I loved my coffee, that I was oddly addicted to my one big Diet Coke a day, and that I was a nightly wine aficionado.

Have you ever admitted something out loud, felt instantly ashamed, and in that moment, realized that a change needed to be made? It's as if the moment you said it, you realized that things had to be different from here on out. That happened to me.

I didn't realize that coffee, diet sodas, and wine are all well-known diuretics. Although they contain a liquid, they are not effective hydration sources. Of course, it makes sense that alcohol would be dehydrating, but I didn't realize they all zap our bodies of needed moisture. I was surprised that my triad of choices had been potentially *dehydrating* me.

In a straightforward article titled "The Importance of Staying Hydrated," the Harvard Medical School staff points out: "Drinking fluids is crucial to staying healthy and maintaining the function of every system in your body, including your heart, brain, and muscles. Fluids carry nutrients to your cells, flush bacteria from your bladder, and prevent constipation."[2] Think of that first statement: *every* system. Wow.

As you know, when we talk about well-being, customization is key. Dr. Julian Seifter, a kidney specialist and associate professor of medicine at Harvard who is quoted in the article, points out that a healthy person needs 30 to 50 ounces of fluid per day (about 1 to 1.5 liters), but he also mentions that the ideal amount varies person to person, and it depends on factors such as age, medications taken, and health issues like kidney and heart function.[3] That makes sense. We will talk a lot in this book about the importance of determining what is right for *you*.

From another article, "The Importance of Hydration for Body and Skin," which was published online by Perricone MD, I learned "given that our bodies are made up of more than 50% water, it probably comes as no surprise that good ol' H_2O is one of the most important energy sources for your body." In fact, water can help you maintain weight, fight fatigue, slow the aging process, reduce high blood pressure and high cholesterol, and flush toxins.[4] I had never really thought that water could *provide* energy, and it gave me a fresh, new perspective.

Together, my doctor and I came up with a much healthier hydration plan. I would measure out and drink eight glasses a day of pure, clean water. As I mentioned, I am not a big fan of plain water, so I agreed to try it with a slice of lemon or lime. (That amount of water was lessened later on because of my kidney issue.) If I ever felt that I had to have coffee, I would only drink decaf coffee, and much less of it. I would never touch a Diet Coke again. Wine would be a rare treat.

I could tell by his tone that he thought I was a strong person, and that I could do this. I knew in my heart that I needed to give this my best effort.

Because I immediately missed the morning's hot beverage in my hands, I did some research and decided to increase my consumption of unsweetened organic green tea. According to my research, green tea is known as "arguably one of the most famous superfoods out there"[5] because of the high levels of antioxidants (polyphenols) and compounds (catechins), which reduce the formation of free radicals in the body. By far my favorite hydration upgrade, I still drink three or four cups of steaming green tea each day.

I executed this exact plan for the next few years until there were no signs of disease in my body. Even today, years later, I keep this overall plan in place. Although I can't prove it, I like to imagine that, at some level, the switch to healthy beverages helped wash the diseases out.

THE *HYDRATE* SPOKE AND WEALTH-BEING

What did creating and committing to my *Hydrate* spoke do for me? By finally giving my body the hydration it was obviously needing, this spoke's positive personal outcome on the Wealth-Being Wheel was, surprisingly, aliveness. I felt fresher drinking clear liquids rather than the murky coffee and the Diet Coke. Did I have a headache for a day or so as my body got off the caffeine? Yes. However, that headache truly motivated me at that point, because I realized the intense hook these beverages had on me. I wanted to be free.

I felt more naturally alive, because I wasn't artificially awake and functioning because of the intense caffeine boosts. I felt more in control, more balanced, and less jumpy around my daughters and friends.

I also felt more aliveness because I began to sleep so much better. I mentioned in the *Get Enough Sleep* spoke that I hadn't realized that wine had been disrupting my sleep, causing me to wake up at 3:00 A.M. That all vanished.

As far as positive professional outcomes on the Wealth-Being Wheel, my *Hydrate* spoke provides better thought leadership, because I am so much more even-keeled. I can think better. I am not distracted. I am not jacked up artificially only to slump before lunch, only to get juiced up again with caffeine. My energy is consistent. I feel more confident in my business decisions, because my mind isn't racing around. I am grounded in exactly the next right thing to do.

Are you ready to experience this really worthwhile upgrade? This one is very straightforward. Let's go.

CUSTOMIZING THE *HYDRATE* SPOKE FOR YOU

1. Let's assess what you drink every day. Make a log for a typical day, and note what you're drinking and how much and when—those three things. Does this provide any insight? What motivates you to drink this beverage at this time in this amount? So much of this is habit. It's amazing what we can drink mindlessly while we are working at our desk.

2. If it makes sense for you, have a knowledgeable doctor help you determine what would be the ideal amount of water for you on a daily basis. Be sure to take any health issues into account.

3. As you try that water recommendation, and you space out your water intake, see how your body *feels*. Does it feel healthy? Does it feel like too much? Let your doctor know if anything seems off; perhaps a modification is necessary. This is a good time for partnership.

4. If you don't like water (there are a lot of us who don't), try sparkling water, or fruit-flavored, unsweetened water.

5. Choose some upgrades. If you already drink water, could you drink filtered, purified water? If you drink regular tea, could you upgrade to organic, so that there are no pesticides in your cup? In the best-case scenario, your tea choice should contain 100 percent organic green tea leaves and no additives.

6. Do you drink sugary soda? Diet soda? Even if it's diet, there are vast amounts of research on how soda has little nutritional value, not to mention the load of artificial sweeteners. Can you let it go? It's a good time to do that. It really is.

7. If you drink alcohol, are you drinking to *get by*, or are you drinking only once in a while to celebrate? Really look into your motivation and see if you can make an upgrade here. If you have an alcohol addiction and you could benefit from professional help, get it. Your well-being is worth it.

8. Stock your fridge and cupboards with your new upgrades. Make sure they are always on hand. (I have more than eight boxes of my favorite organic tea in my cabinet, so that I don't run out.) It's when we run out that we are pulled back to our old bad habits.

9. Make sure that you bring your healthier beverages with you. Bring the sparkling water in the car or pack your tea choice in your pocket or briefcase. Have it on your person for ease of execution!

INCREDIBLE WELL-BEING CUSTOMIZATIONS FROM AN EXCEPTIONAL EXECUTIVE

Kara Goldin, Founder and CEO, Hint, Inc.

Kara Goldin says she has had a long-held theory that "we are our own worst enemies. We put up our own walls."

Oftentimes, she notes, people are entrapped by the words "I can't." Kara's signature vibe, if she encounters a problem, is "That is really interesting," or "Give me the puzzle to go solve."

And solve she does. Amongst her friends, her 145-plus employees, who bustle between the four buildings at the Hint company headquarters on San Francisco's Union Street, and her audiences, Kara is an inspirational kick-starter.

Kara is the ideal messenger on how we can become our own best advocate instead of being our own worst enemy. She recently spoke to a crowd of 5,000 employees at Humana, where she talked about business agility, about creating a new mind-set, and about reinvention. A commanding speaker, she has presented to numerous audiences, more than ever in the last two years, including a *Wall Street Journal* business panel, a keynote address at HustleCon, and a speech to employees at Chobani, Oracle, Instagram, and LinkedIn.

In the midst of the internet golden years, Kara rose to become AOL's youngest female vice president of electronic commerce and shopping, which she built into a billion-dollar division. After she had three children, and while she contemplated her next business move, she struggled to lose all the baby weight, became plagued with terrible adult acne, and suffered from an acute lack of energy that she couldn't fully blame on being a new mom. With no medical diagnosis forthcoming, Kara took a hard look at the 8 to 12 Diet Cokes she was consuming every day. Having harbored the habit for years, she simply assumed, like many people, that diet drinks were better for her than regular soda.

Initially, she looked at the soda's ingredient label and realized that she didn't know any of the chemicals right off the bat. She explains,

"So out of not really understanding, I thought, 'I will just put this aside for now.' " She decided to switch to plain water. "I am not saying it was easy," she admits, "but when I set my mind to something, I just go for it."

To her amazement, *with this single change*, she found that she became "one hundred percent more detoxed." She dropped 55 pounds in 6 months, cleared up her skin entirely, and completely regained her energy.

She says that switching to water—that simple yet profoundly health-enhancing shift—taught her that she "could actually change [her] life significantly." She had gone from being her own worst enemy to her own greatest advocate.

There was only one challenge with her new hydration strategy: she found drinking plain water to be unbearably dull. She explains, "I aspire to be a water drinker. I never was." To add excitement and variety, she started taking fruit, putting it on the stove, boiling it down, and borrowing the medicine dropper from her kids' liquid Tylenol to add two or three fruit essence drops to her bottle of water. She says, "This strategy allowed me to drink more water because I wasn't as bored." She thought that others might feel the same way, and she noticed a gaping hole in the marketplace for this alternative.

With her characteristic sense of burning curiosity, she simultaneously began to read, interview people, and learn everything she could about diet drinks: why they had affected her so terribly, how the commonly used chemicals may cause havoc on your system, how your body and brain detrimentally react to sweetness in general, and how these drinks are target-marketed. She concluded that she has an acute sensitivity to many of the diet sweeteners. Even today, she is so sensitive that she can actually smell stevia, and she gets an immediate headache from erythritol, which belongs to a processed class of compounds called sugar alcohols.

Kara studied traditional sugar drinks as well, even those infused with vitamins, and learned that often, drinks marketed as healthier alternatives to Coke or Pepsi often have even *more* sugar.

Determined to create a healthier alternative—a no-sweetener, no-preservative, zero-calorie, real-fruit-flavored water—for lots of other people besides her family, Kara didn't stop until Hint, Inc. was born. Fast forward to 2019. With Kara as CEO and her attorney husband as COO, Hint Inc., she says proudly, is "the largest, independent, nonalcoholic beverage company in the United States." And, she adds, with emphasis, "We really care about consumer health. It's the customer's right to understand what products are ultimately doing or not doing to them."

Hint, Inc. has more than $100 million in annual revenue, with the company selling Hint Water, Hint Sparkling, and Hint Kick (all vegan, gluten-free, soy and nut free, and NON-GMO certified). Also important to her, the bottles have a BPA-free lining. Hint also has a new breakout sunscreen line, made with the same fruit essences, which are oxybenzone and paraben-free. Kara is passionate about helping people lead the healthiest life possible.

She's passionate about her own health too, and she drinks between 8 to 20 bottles of Hint water a day. Laughing, she notes, "I am always drinking water." In fact, she may be the most well-hydrated Exceptional Executive that we have.

She encourages her staff to drink water too, and glass door fridges packed with Hint water are within easy reach. She says, "The running joke at Hint is that once you start working here, you have to go to the bathroom all the time." She adds that once people's systems get detoxed, their bodies crave the water, but the bathroom runs diminish.

She notes that most competitive modern offices provide employees with a lineup of complimentary espresso and coffee, sugar and diet sodas, and even Red Bulls, but Hint is making its way into many offices as a healthier option. Currently, they are the largest beverage provider in health-conscious Silicon Valley.

Kara believes that many employees reach for the default options their employers offer, and that, unfortunately, "it's something they aren't really paying attention to." She believes that if employees were offered a healthier choice, like pure, fruit-essence water, they would jump at the chance. At Google, one of their biggest customers, where the communal fridges are stocked with Hint, the company's many "Hint Hoarders" are known to grab their favorite flavors. On her first big delivery to the company, every bottle of Hint vanished in the first day.

Because healthy hydration is such a crucial part of optimal functioning, she says that "employers get more productivity, less sick days, greater health overall, and lots and lots of change." She says that in the best possible scenario, the company commits to a healthier workforce from the CEO level, human resources level, and the insurance level. These are the coordinated conversations that higher-level companies are having.

After Kara got Hint into Whole Foods and many other corporations, she noticed an encouraging trend: during the first five years that she personally handled the company's customer service, she received email after email thanking her for creating a product that had such a tremendously positive impact. She says, "How many times are they writing to a large soda company thanking them for solving their company's health problems?" Probably never.

She's proud here. On a meta level, she says, "I am a big believer that everyone should have access to clean water. Absolutely, that is my thing." Deeply affected by the Flint, Michigan, lead-laden water crisis, she's motivated to make sure all children, regardless of income, have access to safe and clean water, and the company now has a lobbyist working with them to explore possibilities, be it cleaning up school drinking fountains or offering more choices than milk or chocolate milk in school lunches. She simply adds, "Everyone has a right to stay hydrated."

So for any people who are their own greatest enemy or who are inclined to say "I can't," Kara feels anything is possible. Looking around her bustling headquarters, she says, "None of this was supposed to happen." She never intended to be a consumer-packaged goods entrepreneur or executive; she simply said "I can" to an incredible opportunity to promote positive outcomes. She credits one trait that has been with her since college: that burning desire to "go do great stuff every day that could actually create some kind of change."

For those of us wanting to make a positive change today or this minute, could drinking pure, clean water be one of the best things we could possibly do?

Kara doesn't even pause. "One hundred percent!"

Relax: Taking It (Very) Easy

"Each person deserves a day away in which no problems are confronted, no solutions searched for. Each of us needs to withdraw from the cares which will not withdraw from us."[1]

—Maya Angelou

CHAINED

The massage therapy room glowed with the cozy golden cast of the Himalayan salt lamp. A small river rock fountain trickled peacefully in the corner, the massage table was covered with a tan velour blanket as soft as a teddy bear, and the corner of the blanket was folded over, an inviting envelope for me to slide into.

I was finally going to bring relaxation into my healing journey. My illness was somewhat improving from the changes I had made to the first five BODY spokes, but it was still stubbornly in place, and the decision to focus on relaxation seemed like the perfect next thing to do, guided even. My first massage hadn't started yet, but already I knew it was going to be healing.

Was there any better feeling than the moment when I nestled my head into the cushy face cradle, took a deep sigh of relief, and acknowledged that there was an entire hour of Swedish deep-tissue massage ahead of me? Could anything be more luxurious? More welcome in that moment? I didn't think so.

I took an extra moment to carefully place my cell phone under my right hip, and luckily, it sank into the plush massage table so that my hips were somewhat even. It was on vibrate, and I thought, proudly, "How genius I am that I won't miss anything important this way. If someone texts or calls, I can easily sneak a peek." I was sure the massage therapist would barely notice, and I was certain that other customers did that all the time.

Well, the massage therapist did notice, and people don't usually do that. After the third time I peeked at my phone, mid-massage, saying, "Oh, whoops, just a second!" he stepped back and said, somewhat softly and possibly annoyed, "Why don't you let me put that over here?" He pointed at a low shelf no more than two feet away.

"Oh, I couldn't," I told him. "What if someone needs me?"

I looked in his eyes and made a quick assessment. He was in his twenties, and I figured that he just didn't realize the on-all-the-time responsibility that goes with pursuing a newly rising career, handling illnesses, and being the mom of two very small girls while their dad is away on business. That phone was chained to me, always. I needed to be available.

He responded with a level of concern for me, an unexpected tenderness that I hadn't experienced in a long time. He had been massaging one of my arms, and he held one of my hands up. It was so badly swollen from the rheumatoid arthritis that it was almost twice the normal size.

He said, ""Look at your hands," but what I heard him really say, was *"Look at what you are doing to yourself."*

I reluctantly gave him my phone and felt odd, conflicted, incomplete, and out of sorts. I wasn't worried about my pile of clothes or jewelry right there next to it. However, I could feel the phone's palpable pull, and I peeked at it out of the corner of my eye.

Halfway through the massage, he asked me to flip onto my back, so that I was looking up at the ceiling. When he began massaging the back of my neck, he was completely cradling my head in his hands. I don't know if I had ever had anyone hold the weight of my head like that. Completely new to me, his hands felt as nurturing as a mother, as comforting as God's, as if he were taking all my responsibilities away. Not a thing to do, I just let the heaviness of my head rest there. I don't remember *ever in my life* feeling that feeling.

I couldn't stop the tears from pouring down the sides of my face and into my ears.

MELTING INTO THE *RELAX* SPOKE

I worked with this same skilled massage therapist every week for the next five years, and I learned how to completely relax, forget everything, give myself that gift of an hour, and totally unplug.

How had I even gotten to that point, at my first massage with my cell phone under my hip? For those of us who are "challenged relaxers," introspection is key.

First, as a perfectionist and an achiever, part of my issue was that I felt I didn't deserve to relax. There was always so much to do, either with clients when I was at work, or with my daughters when we were home, and I just felt that I needed to keep moving so that I had even the slightest chance of getting the most important things done. Because I always felt behind and reactive, I didn't feel that I had earned the right to unwind.

Second, as an ardent list maker, I would think I could do and check off *just one more thing*, even if I approached blinding exhaustion. I could send that research report to the treasured client or put away that piled laundry. This "one more thing" habit prevented me from ever relaxing.

What was the solution for this? For me, it was to shift into a mind frame of deserving and worthiness. I really had to learn that *I deserve a break*.

I learned (the hard way) that the more you work, the more critical it is to do the complete opposite. In other words, the more stressed you are, the more important it is to de-stress.

You might be surprised at how many executives and entrepreneurs have told me that they relax by exercising, especially running. They say their stress melts away as they jog their familiar route. I love that this happens for them, but I would not call it relaxing; to me, it is more akin to *Enlivening Exercise* from Spoke 3, and here, we are talking about totally relaxing, unplugging, taking it easy, giving ourselves a much-deserved break.

I hate to admit this, and it makes me cringe now, but back then, relaxing felt downright *unproductive*. I hadn't a clue about the benefits. How did it make sense to just do *nothing*? Why didn't I just use the time for something that would dig me out of my hole of being overwhelmed? And thus, the vicious cycle continued.

Psychotherapist Barton Goldsmith, PhD, writes, "It doesn't matter what form your idle time takes, as long as it's not destructive. You owe yourself the gift of a deep breath and a view of the long sunset. And if you tell yourself that you are being unproductive, remember that you can't function well if you've exhausted all your resources by never stopping to take a rest."[2]

Relaxation is a crucial lever in stress management, and the Mayo Clinic cites multiple benefits to our bodies, including slowing our heart and breathing rates, lowering blood pressure, improving digestion, reducing the activity of stress hormones, reducing muscle tension and chronic pain, improving sleep quality, lowering fatigue, reducing anger and frustration, and boosting confidence to handle problems.[3] Sign us up for every single one, right?

Many of these benefits have been widely known for centuries. Even the ancient Greek historian Herodotus, born around 425 B.C., believed that "if a man insisted always on being serious, and never allowed himself a bit of fun and relaxation, he would go mad or become unstable without knowing it."[4]

So the key for me was to start relaxing. My body was screaming for help, and at this point in my well-being journey, this was something I hadn't tried yet. The criteria? Very simple: an activity (or really inactivity) where I put forth little to no effort.

I began experimenting and soon found myself looking forward to the weekly massages, and excited to book manicures and pedicures.

THE *RELAX* SPOKE AND WEALTH-BEING

This *Relax* spoke is a commitment to self-care, to revival, to regrouping, and really, to self-love and appreciation. If I need encouragement even today, my words to myself are "you deserve this."

As far as positive personal outcomes on the Wealth-Being Wheel, I began to feel, for the first time in my life, a sense of calm. Whenever I relaxed, I felt a newfound sense of peace, and for lack of a better word, an absence of worry. That in itself was an immense gift—an hour or even a few moments without my pressing cares. I noticed that with my body at rest, my mind soon followed. No longer forced to be on high alert all the time, my physical body took a huge sigh of relief. My mind turned off, and I felt lighter and more observant.

I believe my weekly massages had a tremendously soothing effect on my chronic pain, literally working out the tension, and over time I began to notice the pain subsiding. Who knows how much of the physical pain that I was experiencing was tied to my emotions?

As far as positive professional outcomes on the Wealth-Being Wheel, my *Relax* spoke, to my great surprise, led me to peak performance. I thought taking a break would make me fall behind in my work, but instead, it revived me so that I was more productive, more rejuvenated, and more easily able to deliver excellence. I stopped cramming so many client meetings into one day (I used to think that was efficient). Instead, I started to spread them out, to allow for a substantial break. Those breaks, maybe sitting at a coffee shop daydreaming for 20 minutes, acted like a professional palate cleanser, a totally refreshing reboot.

Are you ready to relax and experience this immensely important spoke? You deserve it.

CUSTOMIZING THE *RELAX* SPOKE FOR YOU

1. Currently, what are your favorite ways to relax? What do you like to do to unplug and recharge? List a handful that resonate with you.
2. If your list is sparse or nonexistent (and you wouldn't be the first!), think of one relaxing thing that you could add. If you are stuck for ideas, consider adding "listening to music," but make sure you choose songs that melt your cares away as opposed to revving you up. Another simple idea that you can do almost anywhere is to sit quietly (outside is optimal) and set a timer for 10 minutes.
3. I suggest that you actually book time on your schedule to relax—each week of course, but ideally each day. Especially if you are not used to prioritizing this, you may have to *manipulate* yourself into taking a breather. (I had to do this with my massage appointments; I couldn't cancel within 24 hours, and on certain days, that limitation actually forced me to go.) Can you schedule an appointment for this crucial spoke into your calendar?
4. If you are prone to workaholism (and again, you wouldn't be the first), I suggest getting an accountability partner for this project. Tell a colleague or loved one that you're planning to relax this week or this afternoon, and check in with that person to confirm that you actually followed through.

For someone who rarely stops, this spoke can be *tremendously* difficult to implement. Not stopping is a hard habit to break. It's harder than it sounds, but the benefits are better than you can imagine.

INCREDIBLE WELL-BEING CUSTOMIZATIONS FROM AN EXCEPTIONAL EXECUTIVE

Yanik Silver, Founder and CEO, Maverick1000; Serial Entrepreneur

Yanik Silver was one of the first people to buy a $200,000 future flight ticket to suborbital space aboard Virgin Galactic Airways, and he's already done several zero-gravity prep trainings for the flight. On one of his free evenings, he performed a live stand-up comedy sketch for a packed audience at The Improv in Washington, DC. Another time, he broke 200 miles per hour driving a racecar with nothing but a green Speedo on.

If you are thinking Yanik already sounds like the furthest thing from a person who relaxes, think again. To begin, he says that in general, "I'm pretty laid-back." But digging deeper, it's worth noting that Yanik makes conscious space for it all. Like many high-achieving entrepreneurs, he has a rock-solid work ethic and admits, "I don't want to fall short of my potential." On the other hand, he also believes that the bigger the future vision you have for yourself, the bigger energy renewal you are going to need.

Yanik thinks of relaxation as a form of surrender to the serendipitous. He explains, "I believe things happen for a reason in the right way. The more you push, the more it's your ego trying to make it the way you want it. It has been a learning process for me to allow things to show up." For him, the best word to describe this allowing and surrender is *play*.

He believes that "play is called 're/creation' for a reason," because "play is one of our most natural expressions of who we are in our perfected states. Joy and play are totally interwoven together. When we play there is a youthful energy and spark to us that can be seen by everyone. As adults we've gotten too serious. When you allow the little boy or girl inside of you to play, magic happens. The word 're/creation' gives us a clue about the power of play. The words are re/creation because it 'recreates' our world."

"Plus," he adds, "the most evolved people I know are the most fun and playful."

How did this fun-loving, curious, and open spirit come to appreciate the value of play? It helps to understand his career trajectory, and we'll go from there.

The son of Russian immigrant parents who came to the United States when he was three, Yanik's first huge successes were on his own in digital content, digital marketing, and digital publishing, and he successfully bootstrapped and self-funded eight different product and service ideas to reach the seven-figure sales mark.

He created and hosted one of the most highly regarded, live educational and networking events for this market, called The Underground Online Seminar, which drew 500-plus entrepreneurs yearly from around the globe and sold out every year for 10 years. An absolute visionary in the space, Yanik was named one of *Entrepreneur Magazine*'s top 50 Online Marketing Influencers.

When it was time to take everything to the next level, he gathered his business acumen, penchant for wild adventures, commitment to having something charitable mixed in, and his overarching desire to "combine everything I really liked together," and in 2007, he founded Maverick1000. The company is a private, invitation-only global collective of top entrepreneurs and visionary industry leaders who meet for breakthrough retreats, rejuvenating adventures, and impact opportunities. With seven to eight unique experiences and retreats a year to choose from, these leaders meet, as Yanik says in short, with the goal to "make more, have more fun, and give more." The goal is to bring together 1,000 game-changing entrepreneurs. He says, "The idea is to light one thousand 'suns' who can each ignite another one thousand suns."

The impact aspect of Maverick1000 matters a lot to Yanik, and he's driven "to figure out where I can make a difference." To that end, 10 percent of Maverick member fees go directly to an impact fund, and to date the group has raised more than $3 million in charitable contributions that benefit entrepreneurship worldwide. Yanik helps the group direct entrepreneur brainpower and resources to cause partners, key projects, and ideas. For instance, on one of their impact trips to Haiti, the group created a for-profit small business whose proceeds help fund Hope2Haiti's work with orphanages.

And Yanik gets even more "meta" than that. His lifetime goal is to connect visionary leaders to create business models and new ideas for solving 100 of the world's most impactful issues by the year 2100. To guide entrepreneurs who are set on solving with him, he wrote his best-selling book, *The Evolved Enterprise: An Illustrated Guide to Re-Think, Re-Imagine & Re-Invent Your Business to Deliver Meaningful Impact and Even Greater Profits.*[5]

So with all this on his plate, why is unplugging so important to him? He recalls an analogy from a friend about how we don't feel guilty recharging our phones at the end of the day. In contrast, he says, "Even when we take days off, there's definitely a level of guilt that happens around how we should be out there hustling twenty-four-seven, and there's this notion of hustle that has become a thing. I don't believe in hustle necessarily. I believe in alignment and intention."

So what does he do in his rejuvenating off time? He says that when he unplugs and recharges, he looks for and finds "joy in play," and he's often delighted that "surprising new paths open up."

His favorite alone, down-time practice is journaling, which he does every evening before bed. It helps him clear his mind, a benefit he describes as "huge, because as entrepreneurs, as busy executives, and as leaders, we have a lot floating around inside our head." He explains, "Whatever I start with is not usually what I end up with. It creates a beginning, middle, and end, because it forces you to come to a con-clusion in some way, shape, or form before you get to the end of the page." One of his favorite things to do is take his journal and go back serendipitously, noting great ideas and insights. He adds, "I love it."

In his journal, he layers another favorite play element, which is draw-ing. When he was a young kid, he wanted to be a cartoonist, so much so that he snuck out of the house at age five to buy markers with his Hanu-kah money. Some of his doodles are meaningful phrases (like "Everyday

Funday"), mandala shapes, labyrinths, and diagrams, while others are cartoons with a cosmic flair.

His next book will be a colorful compilation of these journal entries and drawings, interconnected by theme and creativity, which he says best could be described as the "Galactic Instruction Manual" he wished he'd had all along.

He loves relaxing with his loving wife, Missy, and playing with his school-aged children, Zack and Zoe, so when he's not traveling, he frequently works from home so he can be available when they come home in the afternoons. One practice here that has made a huge difference is being fully present with whatever he's doing. He explains, "If you are going to play ball with your kid, go play ball. Because if you are doing something, actually do it and be there." During these times, he turns off his laptop and his phone. He explains, "The world won't explode if you are not able to respond immediately." For those of us tied to electronics, he says that breaking this habit during your downtime is "incredibly liberating."

Yanik enjoys recharging among friends, who are often Maverick members. He says that this relaxed time together has tremendous value because of "the humanness, the realness, the authenticity." He advises, "Be playful! You don't need this business façade. There's this intermeshing now, and people want real people to work with that they can trust." He adds, "We even have a name for it: Maverick Moments. It could be a big 'a-ha' or insight, and a lot of times it is something that happened where everyone was just laughing hysterically. It just connects people in a deep way."

One such moment? Yanik and Sir Richard Branson were doing a private Q&A session for the Maverick group at an "Under the Sea"–themed party on Necker Island, where they were focusing on advocacy for the ocean. To have a little fun, Yanik's business team presented the two men with full-on mermaid tails to wear. A few minutes later, they both donned the colorful tails, took their shirts off, and continued taking questions!

His advice for us? Yanik reminds us that "work expands to the amount of time we give to it." Therefore, he says, we need "to give ourselves permission to explore how to play, to draw on what we loved as kids, and to think about how to add more of this to our lives." He suggests going as far as setting an appointment for yourself—your own "playdate." He advises, "When you have the choice between two options, consider what brings out more play, more joy."

Whether you do this relaxing play alone, with family, or with friends, he says that it opens you up to serendipitous moments packed with meaning. He explains, "I love what shows up, and there is always a very intriguing opening for me to see that it's not just me pushing and pushing, but where is the flow of life taking me?"

He concludes, "To me, that playfulness and joy are all inseparable. And joy is your path back home."

PART TWO

Universal MIND
Spokes

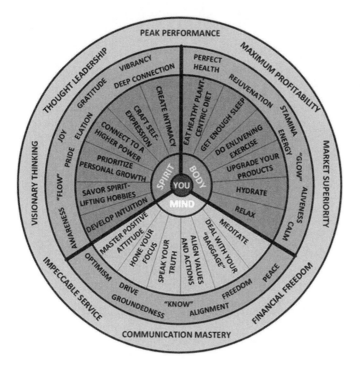

Meditate: For the Mind that Veers Between Om and Oops!

"The quieter you become, the more you can hear."[1]
—Baba Ram Dass

INFREQUENT PIT STOPS

With my multiple health crises, my "falling knives" were truly terrifying me, and I desperately reached for any and all insight into how I might possibly heal myself. I was also facing the obvious truth that my six Well-Being Wheel BODY practices hadn't fully healed me yet: I was still in chronic pain every single day. I had an overwhelming, depressing sense of "now what?"

One day I set my hopes for an easy answer from the stars. To that end, I scheduled a custom phone reading with one of the world's most respected Vedic astrologers, Bill Levacy. With three published books on this 5,000-year-old astrologic system, dozens of awards and a raving recommendation from one of my friends, Bill caught my attention and garnered an hour slot on my calendar.

Right off the bat, I asked him if I was *destined* to be sick. He responded with something I will never forget: "You are *destined* to understand the consequences of running a racecar around the track without a pit stop." I gulped.

Then he added, *"The power is in the stopping."*

A week later, I was in San Francisco at the UCSF Osher Center for Integrative Medicine, seeing one of their lead alternative MDs for further insight on my diet and supplements. He noticed I was glancing at my vibrating cell phone every so often. He asked, "Do you meditate?"

I answered, "No, not ever."

On a prescription pad sheet, he wrote down Jack Kornfield's name; a book title, *A Path With Heart*;[2] as well as *Spirit Rock Meditation Center*, which is an hour north of the city. I had driven by the location dozens of times on vacation weekends and seen the modest wooden sign at the base of some gorgeous hills, but I had never given it a moment's thought.

On another prescription pad sheet, he wrote down Jon Kabat-Zinn's name, and another book title, *Full Catastrophe Living*.[3] My heart sunk. Without any idea of the title's reference, I cynically thought to myself, "This is what it has come to: my life is a catastrophe!" When I later learned that the subtitle is *Using the Wisdom of Your Body and Mind to Face Stress, Pain, and Illness*, I knew why he'd recommended it.

I do believe in signs, and the coincidence and timing of such similar, targeted advice from two very different experts—an astrologer and a medical doctor—was not lost on me. In these two enlightened moments, I grudgingly realized I needed to enter new territory, and I needed a MIND section of the Well-Being Wheel. I was committed to doing whatever it took to be well again.

THE RISE OF THE UNIVERSAL *MEDITATE* SPOKE

I mentioned before that a great education will teach you how to research things, and I find it humorous looking back that I formulated my *Meditate* spoke with the vigor of a businesswoman with a deadline (ASAP, right?), the curiosity of a sleuth uncovering a complex mystery, and the desperation of a very sick person who thinks this might be just the thing to turn it all around.

What I surprisingly discovered is that my *Meditate* spoke, in its highest, most noble form, was not about DOING but about BEING.

At the time, I had no idea how important the two "prescribed" meditation teachers—Jack Kornfield and Jon Kabat-Zinn—would become to me, or that I would see them both speak live for the next 10-plus years, hanging onto their every word. Kornfield, a former Buddhist monk trained in Thailand, is an internationally known meditation teacher, one of the key people to introduce Buddhist mindfulness to the West, and cofounder of the Spirit Rock Meditation Center in Woodacre, California. Kabat-Zinn is an internationally known meditation teacher engaged in bringing mindfulness to society and medicine, the author of numerous books, and a professor emeritus of the University of Massachusetts Medical School.

Prepared to tackle my meditation project with the same determination I poured into my work each day, I scoured their books, marking relevant passages with multiple Post-it notes, colored flags, and copious underlining. I then tried three different types of meditation: sitting, walking, and gazing. Here is how each type resonated with me and what adjustments I needed to make.

I learned a simple sitting meditation: sitting in a chair with my feet grounded on the floor and my eyes closed, focusing on my breathing and aiming for a calmness and ease. Seems simple, right? No, for me, it was the most difficult thing to do.

For one, I could not bear to meditate sitting up, because, not surprisingly, the pain in my body seemed exponentially worse when I sat there, trying to breathe and calm myself. I noticed every little hurt, amplified, and the feelings in my knees, feet, and hands would scream at me, almost as if to say "notice me!" Both teachers recommend staying with it anyway, explaining that this is a normal experience that is part of the process, but I just couldn't do it.

For this reason, I capitulated and took to meditating lying down, and even at Jack Kornfield's daylong retreat at his center, there I was in the very back of the room, trying to be invisible, flat-out on a blanket with cushions under my knees and a pillow under my head. As I reflect back, I am sure that literally I couldn't bear to look head-on at my life—it was just too painful—and it was easier to "take" it lying down. I must have looked like a patient in a hospital back there, and in a sense, I was. However, ultimately, I found it to be very relaxing, lying there, simply breathing in and out, cultivating my awareness, and noting what arises. In fact, I continue to do it now for 10 to 20 minutes, twice a day, morning and night. I call it "beditating."

I get a lot of flak from more serious meditators, who laugh and tell me I can't possibly do this and not fall asleep. I wink and say, "Don't judge!" This is my customization, and I am sticking to it!

Fortunately for me, during Jack's daylong retreat, we alternated with a walking meditation, which is simply slowly walking on a chosen path about 10 to 30 paces in length, with a goal of cultivating awareness and alert presence. As with the sitting meditation, the idea is to harness your wandering mind and bring it back, in this case instead of the breath, to the step at hand. I LOVE walking meditations, and it seems like a good customization for the on-the-move, hard-to-settle energy that seems inherent to my body. My favorite place to do this form of meditation is on my backyard patio. It has about 20 paces back and forth, and the surrounding Zen vibe of my yard is perfect.

Finally, I have added a real favorite, a gazing meditation, to my customizations for this spoke. Loosely based on a Tibetan technique called "sky gazing," it's a way of connecting your gaze with the natural world.

I simply head to my backyard sanctuary, where I feel most at home in the world. I sit comfortably in one of the ironwork rocking chairs and stare at my hummingbird feeder, where there are always dodging, brilliant hummers, my spirit animal. I breathe deeply, notice their beauty, and feel the power in the stopping.

THE *MEDITATE* SPOKE AND WEALTH-BEING

What did implementing my *Meditate* spoke do for me? By giving my whirlwind mind a moment's rest, *I was invited toward* (notice my language) this spoke's positive personal outcome on the Wealth-Being Wheel: peace. I saw only a glimmer of this at first; it's not like I was suddenly awash with peace after my first session, but there were some encouraging signs almost immediately.

I began to know what calm felt like. Sadly, it had been many years—probably during my high school days—since I had felt true calmness. This realization clicked after a number of doctor's appointments where the nurse would take my blood pressure and then, for kicks, I would do a quick 20-second sitting meditation and have the nurse take it a second time. Consistently, there was a significant drop (about 10 points) in the top *and* bottom numbers. It was amazing. The nurse always commented, "Wow, you should do that more!"

Another benefit is that I absolutely appear more calm to others. Before my *Meditate* spoke, I remember running late and hustling my oldest daughter, who was about five years old at the time, to her speech therapy appointment. She paused slowly and pointed up to the sky, showing me a gorgeous rainbow. With my head down, lost in my angry thoughts about the traffic and everything on my list of to-do items, I never would have noticed it. Meditation helped me break that cycle of DOING so that I could BE a better mom and person.

One of my best friends, Juliana, says that I am so much calmer now than 10 years ago that I am "barely recognizable." She says I used to appear constantly rushed but now I seem to be, in her words, "totally present." Wow.

As far as positive professional outcomes on the Wealth-Being Wheel, my *Meditate* spoke has brought me so much more visionary thinking in my career than I ever thought possible. Since I never took a moment to stop beforehand, I never was able to cultivate the openness required for inspired, strategic thinking. Although I had always been successful, I had no idea what I was really missing.

As I cultivate meditative awareness, whether beditating, walking, or gazing, I really try to empty my mind, and quite brilliant things have drifted by, such as the title for this book, the name of an executive who would be truly inspiring to interview, a unique way of explaining something to a wealth management client, or a funny example for an upcoming keynote speech. I am not trying to *think* of my career—I am always bringing my attention back to my breath—but the stopping has had a miraculous way of bringing me super-fresh insight.

Are you ready to experience this game-changing spoke? Let's go.

CUSTOMIZING THE *MEDITATE* SPOKE FOR YOU

1. Do you practice any form of meditation now? Do you feel like it works well for you? If yes, let's call that a winning customization for you. Keep doing that!

2. Look through the types of very common meditation practices that I mentioned: sitting meditation, walking meditation, and gazing meditation. (Does beditation count? I think so!) Are there any that resonated with you and that you would like to try? See if you can schedule at least one new type into your busy schedule this week. It's important to act sooner rather than later so that the energy doesn't wane. See what you think. Could it be a new customization for you?

3. Are you inspired to read more about meditation practice? I highly recommend any and all books by Jack Kornfield and Jon Kabat-Zinn, both truly masterful meditation teachers. Other bestselling meditation writers include Pema Chodron and Thich Nhat Hanh.

4. Are you interested in exploring a Meditation app? There are some amazing ones out there that offer everything from guided meditations to soothing nature sounds, and I would be remiss

not to mention some of them, such as *Headspace, 10% Happier, Unplug Meditation,* and *Calm.* These all require paid subscriptions, but they are of superior high quality.

5. Interested in free meditation content? YouTube has a plethora of high-quality guided meditations available. Try one and see if it resonates.

6. Do you have any interest in attending a full meditation day or a multiple-day meditation retreat? Good places to start looking would be the Spirit Rock Meditation Center in California, the Insight Meditation Society in Barre, Massachusetts, and the Chopra Center in California.

INCREDIBLE WELL-BEING CUSTOMIZATIONS FROM AN EXCEPTIONAL EXECUTIVE

Rich Fernandez, Cofounder, Wisdom Labs, and CEO, Search Inside Yourself Leadership Institute

At 5:00 a.m., Rich Fernandez is in his home's private study, alone on his meditation cushion, right in front of the window. It's dark out, but as he settles in, he notices the distant lights of San Francisco outside, and in a way, it connects him to the outer environment. The natural world means a lot to him, even if through a window on a cool foggy morning. He's ready for his daily, dedicated mindfulness practice.

During this first 20-minute sitting meditation, which he describes as an "attention practice," he works on his concentration by focusing on his breath. If his mind wanders, he gently but firmly brings his attention back to his breath, in and out. He is intentionally trying to settle and focus his mind and come to a place of mental clarity by bringing it back to a single object of attention.

He says that skillfully gathering our attention is in itself valuable. In a world that's constantly pulling at our attention, it's helpful to come back to a single point of focus. It creates a sense of mental clarity.

He then alternates to a 10-minute walking meditation, and in his study there is enough room to take about 10 paces back and forth. He says, "In walking, there is an integrative aspect of the mindfulness practice, where insights come in a more freeform fashion." He explains that reflections arise out of the sitting but then germinate a little bit more when doing walking meditation. Since it's a dynamic process, as he walks, "ideas get digested or integrate more fully."

He then embarks on another round of sitting meditation for approximately 20 minutes, first doing an "open reflection exercise" where, he says, "I just let whatever arises arise. I am not grasping for any of it. I am just seeing what comes up—the quality and content of what is coming up, and noticing what is going on in my mind, heart, and body."

After that, he may add a visualization exercise. He sets an intention, such as reflecting on a specific thing in his life or in his career. It could be something challenging, like a difficult negotiation at work, or something wonderful, like playing baseball with his twelve-year-old son, Noah. He spends time paying attention to what arises and visualizing the best possible outcomes.

Last, he may add empathy or compassion practices, in which he cultivates goodwill or good wishes for himself and others.

So for 30 to 60 minutes each day, Rich cycles through all of these practices. Broadly speaking, he summarizes it by explaining that "you settle the mind first and then welcome what's most alive," or in other words, you "cultivate attention and develop awareness." When asked if it's akin to bringing your puppy into the yard and then letting it walk around, he laughs out loud and says, "Yes! That's a beautiful way to describe it!"

A trained psychologist with a PhD in Counseling Psychology and an MA in Organizational Psychology, both from Columbia University, Rich Fernandez was formerly Head of Executive Education at Google, and before that Head of Learning and Organization Development at eBay. He is cofounder of Wisdom Labs, a think tank and leadership consultancy that promotes mindfulness and well-being in organizations. He is also the CEO of Search Inside Yourself Leadership Institute (SIYLI), a nonprofit educational institution that grew to offer Google's mindfulness-based emotional intelligence curriculum to individuals, communities, and organizations around the world. To say that we have an expert in mindfulness, cognitive psychology, and human performance science in our midst would be a huge understatement. Rich is the perfect Exceptional Executive and role model for this *Meditate* spoke.

Rich's morning daily practice starts every day on the right foot, but much more than that, he says that mindfulness is the driving force of his soul, permeating both his personal and professional life, a true source of his Wealth-Being. He describes mindfulness as an "innate human capacity," something that we can all exercise. Rich says the good news is that while it's helpful to do some "dedicated practice, such as meditation or prayer," he notes that "the 'integrated practice'—bringing attention, awareness, and compassion to everyday life activities as you are experiencing them at home and/or work—is also a way to grow mindfulness." Whether Rich is taking a weekend hike, making a farmer's market run with his treasured wife, picking up his son from school and playing catch, or answering a recent WhatsApp message from a friend in Shanghai or Mumbai, mindfulness allows him to be present to what's alive and important to him in a real life way.

As far as his career, he says his daily meditation practices allows him "to be agile and responsive to pretty much all circumstances." The second part of his daily practice, with the open reflection and visualization exercises, can serve as a business meeting with himself, where he "brings the very highest-quality attention and awareness" to a work topic that is getting his attention. As the CEO of a global nonprofit serving a wide variety of organizations, each day brings back-to-back meetings and intense challenges.

If he's facing a difficult, stressful negotiation, for example, his allowed space for mindfulness helps him to see that clearly and not get caught up in the same negative pattern, to rehearse in advance, to be responsive rather than reactive, and to approach it with a level of mental clarity and balance. He says it's the opposite of being passive—or worse, overly reactive—in a situation, because he has prepared for it. He's been able to negotiate many a good outcome this way, and he thinks we could too.

For those of us inspired to move forward with this *Meditate* spoke, Rich says to start modestly and to avoid getting too hung up with ideas of achievement or progress. He emphasizes, "It's not about doing more or achieving more. It's a way of being and connecting awareness to your own experience as you are having it." For someone who has dedicated his being in the world to mindfulness, he says that the idea of mastering meditation or mindfulness "is a difficult one because we are *all* on this human journey. Our attention and awareness is *always* being pulled. We are always falling asleep to what is true and good in our lives."

We can't thank him enough for offering the world, and us, some useful insights and ways of waking up.

Deal with Your "Baggage": Stopping Runaway Roller Coasters

"Rise up nimbly and go on your strange journey to the ocean of meanings."[1]

—Rumi

MIND POISON

I had really committed to my journey into my MIND, eagerly seeking clues for healing. I more keenly noticed my thoughts that came and went, especially when I was out and about alone, doing things like driving to work or in between appointments, snipping roses in my garden, or just relaxing on my patio.

What I noticed, when this heightened self-awareness kicked in, really shocked me.

I noticed that my mind, as if moving in a direction on its own, would veer to certain traumatizing moments of my childhood—moments where I felt most wronged. Much like being strapped into a roller coaster with the heavy bars over my shoulders, heading up the steep incline only to speed down the harrowing tracks, I was there for the ride, unable to escape.

From birth through eighth grade, I grew up in the rural Midwest, in a religiously strict family and community, and the usual consequence for actual or suspected wrongdoing was physical punishment. I knew I was not the only child who lived this reality, but for someone as sensitive and perceptive as I was, it had an amplified effect.

There I would be, in my car in present time, driving to work with the gorgeous Northern California hills on either side of me, and even though the memory's place and time was thousands of miles away and 30 years earlier, it would be right there for me on that roller coaster track, in full color. I would be experiencing all the emotions that went with the long-ago event. The same humiliation coursed through my body, because it wasn't so much the pain as being made an example in front of others. I felt the same terror of not knowing how or when the rage of the much larger adult would strike. I experienced the same injustice and helplessness of a child who couldn't defend herself without repercussion, who, not allowed to say a word, was silenced in an unsafe moment.

I had never before realized that in present time, I inadvertently replayed these moments, and that every time I did, it re-traumatized my body. It was as if literal poison was coursing through my veins. My heart would beat faster, anger would well up, and I hadn't even gotten to work yet.

As American writer Ann Beattie says, "People forget years and remember moments."[2] That was true for me. It was as if these specific memories grew and grew in stature, became giant billboards along that roller coaster ride, and came to represent my whole childhood, while the other thousands of beautiful memories (which I also had) took a back seat. I was stuck in a loop remembering the darkness.

Why was I doing this to myself? It hurt me every time I remembered, and certainly, I immediately realized how destructive to my health it could be. I could drink all the green drinks I wanted—and indeed I had one in my car cup holder every morning—but I knew I wouldn't heal anytime soon with that unhealthy, negative energy invading my body. This awareness shifted my perception instantly, and it brought about a new passion, really compassion, for healing this part of my struggling self.

THE ADDITION OF *THE DEAL WITH YOUR "BAGGAGE"* SPOKE

The sixteenth-century Sufi poet Rumi said, "Stretch your arms and take hold of the cloth of your clothes with both hands. The cure for pain is in the pain."[3] I began a quest to find silence, or peace and resolution, from this "remembering" habit that had been in my life for years. I was committed to stopping that roller coaster.

For me, the first step was self-awareness—of consciously knowing I was doing this. It became an actual spoke when I realized the dire seriousness of this habit and its crushing effect on me.

The second step involved an action plan in the direction of healing.

My sister, Mollie, likes to say that we all have baggage of some sort that we carry with us. Some of us carry heavy backpacks, and some of us have lighter duffel bags. She astutely notes that many of us keep the bags concealed, guarded and protected even, and go about our business. Some of us have been deeply traumatized by people, actual events, or circumstances. Some of us have been able to shed the weight of the tough memories and move forward unencumbered. I wanted that for myself, and it became my goal.

For me, I realized professional help might move me along faster, and did several stints of weekly psychotherapy, where I appreciated the skillful listening and advice of my talented therapist. Her focus was to help me work on ME.

I simultaneously worked with spiritual healers who energetically helped me to heal the wounds I was carrying in my body.

Third, I discovered a groundbreaking book called *You Can Heal Your Life* by Louise Hay. Hay consistently ties emotional trauma to illness, saying, "Resentment, criticism, and guilt are the most damaging patterns."[4] Was trauma the root cause of my chronic illnesses? It would be impossible to prove. What I did know is that the very alive memories could not in any way be helping my well-being.

I was so encouraged to hear Hay's solution-oriented belief: "The past has no power over us. It doesn't matter how long we have had a negative pattern. The point of power is in the present moment. What a wonderful thing to realize! We can begin to be free in this moment."[5]

Between the three sources, I learned that what really mattered was that I was moving from being a helpless victim to being an empowered hero on my own healing path.

Along the way, I thought it would be helpful to my healing to share my perception of those dark memories with the adults responsible. Some victims may feel that a helpful confrontation is in order to provide closure, while for others that idea may be incredibly detrimental (and possibly dangerous). In my case, unfortunately, I didn't experience the recognition or remorse (from them) that I was hoping for, but from the exchange, I realized something critically important: as far as dealing with your baggage, the most important character is YOU. You cannot control the level of consciousness or regret or anything in another human being. What you can control is YOUR reaction to any given situation, YOUR self-compassion, YOUR self-love for the strong warrior you have become. That's where the power is.

Hay teaches that we need to understand that the people who hurt us "were doing the best they could with what they had been taught,"[6] and my forgiveness for these people increased significantly. That doesn't mean their actions were acceptable, but I understood that they were doing *what they were capable of* in those stressful moments.

My healing increased when I learned to open my closed heart and to remember all the *beautiful* memories I had with those same adults—and it was true: from the sunny vacations, funny conversations, cozy holidays, and times they *did* support me. More important, it moved me to focus on the truth of who they are *today*.

Finally, I did a lot of "reframing" work, where I started looking at my traumatic experiences in a more positive, empowered light, as an important element of the successful person I have become today. If that hadn't happened to me, I doubt I would be as grounded, resourceful, aware, and devoted to truth. A counselor told me that sometimes, deeply experiencing something you *don't* want allows you to more consciously create the opposite. No doubt, my entire life today is something undeniably great, something that I created out of love, out of power, and without a single shred of that darkness.

THE *DEAL WITH YOUR "BAGGAGE" SPOKE* AND WEALTH-BEING

As far as positive personal outcomes, as shown in the Wealth-Being Wheel, I experienced freedom. I experienced the freedom to think a new, more inspiring thought, such as an idea about my exciting weekend plans. I powerfully choose my own thoughts carefully. Will I ever forget? Will the memories ever go away? No, but those thoughts are not welcome to rob the peace of my life. I control them—they don't control me. You owe that to yourself too.

Powerfully, I had made a promise to myself when my girls were born, and restated it during this healing time, that I would never repeat behaviors that scared and scarred me as a child. I would end the cycle here. That has been my gift to my girls, to myself, and to a world that needs more peace.

As far as positive professional outcomes on the Wealth-Being Wheel, my *Deal with Your "Baggage"* spoke cleared space in my psyche and in my time. Without resentment, what do we have? We have *possibility* for what could be achieved with an upcoming meeting, that keynote presentation, or that client to help. It's like creating more free time to think differently. With more positive energy running through my body, I show up powerful rather than diminished, and I have been able to arrive more like my highest self, well prepared because I have had more time to think and plan. I would categorize this bonus under peak performance. Yes, yes, and yes!

Are you ready to hunker down and deal with this critical spoke? We are doing some heavy lifting here, but I promise it will be worth it.

CUSTOMIZING THE *DEAL WITH YOUR "BAGGAGE"* SPOKE FOR YOU

1. What's really bothering you? Do you have any bad memories or "mind poison" that steals your peace or crowds your current mental space? What's bubbling up? Write everything down. The awareness of it is an important step.
2. Believe that healing from your baggage is possible. Believe that you can be free. Practice visualizing being without the baggage. Who would you be? What would life be like? I believe there's immense power in putting your intention out into the universe, setting the stage for what you want to manifest.
3. Practice being in the present moment in general. Look at people whom you pass by; listen carefully when people speak to you. When you are driving or alone, practice directing your thoughts to the here and now, to what you are seeing. This prevents you from slipping into past memories.
4. Get as much professional healing support as you need and can afford. You may have to try different therapists or see different coaches to find someone who powerfully resonates with you. Be patient, and you will find the right professional partner to help you move forward.
5. Practice gratitude for what is truly right in your life right now. This helps to diminish the power of the dragging, traumatic thoughts by bringing you back to the truth and the present.
6. Keep a journal of your thoughts and feelings, and start writing how the experience may have *positively* affected you. I know this reframing might seem difficult, especially if you are dealing with something horrific, but think how it has shaped you into who you are today. What positive qualities do you embody as a result? Are you more resilient? Do you have more inner strength? Start focusing on your empowerment.

7. Look into Emotional Freedom Technique (EFT), which helps people let go of negative thoughts, memories, and emotions. I have heard so many people mention how this fascinating, easy-to-learn practice, also referred to as "tapping," has helped them remove lifelong baggage and trauma. The Tapping Solution website[7] has a trove of resources.

INCREDIBLE WELL-BEING CUSTOMIZATIONS FROM AN EXCEPTIONAL EXECUTIVE

Marie Case, Managing Partner, Praemia Group, and Chairman of Board, World Business Academy

Would you like a shining example of how to face a trauma with humanity, grace, and self-compassion—how to honor yourself through the process and to emerge, no *soar*, from the ashes as a much better personal and professional version of yourself? Look no further than Marie Case.

Entirely and incredibly successful in executive consulting, Marie was a standout from the start. In the mid-1980s, she worked with Paul Fireman, founder of Reebok, as he was acquiring Ellese, Boston Whaler, and Rockport. In the mid-1990s, as a VP at CSC Index, she led the Management Transformation practice in Europe, where she consulted over the course of eight years in London for British Petroleum as they acquired and integrated Arco, Amoco, Veba, and Sohio.

Focusing on post-merger and acquisition projects, she and her team navigated the integration of the executive leadership teams. Traveling to three cities a week, and hotel after hotel, she sometimes made it home on the weekend, but other times it wasn't worth the travel time.

As successful as she was, Marie realized that there was something missing. Although not physically ill, she says she sensed her own unhealthiness of running on "ambition and adrenal glands." She was offered partner at age 37, but she explains, "I had all of the success I had ever wanted. I had the title, the 'right' relationships, the gorgeous home, the financial well-being, and as everyone who has been there has discovered, peace and happiness were not in it. While it was true that I had control and authority, I discovered I had little access to inner silence. To being present and to empathy."

Highly self-aware, she tried her first run at meditation at a retreat; the entire week she was there, she had laryngitis, and she laughs at the memory: "I could not utter a word!" The irony of not being able to speak, of being in a position to listen, was not lost on her.

She then spent quite a bit of time with noted spiritual leader, academic, and psychologist Ram Dass. She says, "I was picking up the thread. I had always been interested in spirituality and had studied it quite a bit."

Marie saw an aspect of herself that needed reframing. "I was a leader and I got things done. I had great relationships with people. But I had hit a point where I saw I was too mechanistic—operating in a certain kind of frame of what it means to succeed. I began searching for more inner depth, by which I mean consciousness, awareness, and presence—what I call 'spirituality.' I began to reach for other more integrated role models."

What happened next transformed her into the exact role model she had been looking for: a role model for herself.

In 2005, in the midst of traveling and working all over the world, the prominent structures of her personal life came falling down. Her beloved 19-year-old cat died, her marriage crumbled, and she realized that some of her carefully acquired retirement assets vanished from theft. She describes how she dealt with that reality, saying, "I crashed so hard and allowed myself to feel the depth of my sadness. I fell into the deepest, darkest depression. I had always been so resilient, but I had hit my limit."

Marie had kept in touch with a colleague and friend from five years earlier, Gary, who had left a highly successful career in the corporate world to explore his own deeper understanding of his life and purpose.

In fact, he had ventured straight to India, where he met Sri Sai Kaleshwar, considered to be a living saint, and started studying knowledge from ancient palm leaf books about healing and realization.

What happened next shows the power of caring, coordination, friendship, and fate: Gary coordinated a heartfelt invitation to come to the ashram from one of the guru's top students, Monika, and although Marie was in the middle of a divorce with her finances locked, her dear friend, Faith, bought both of them a plane ticket. Marie learned that an additional friend, Jan, also would be at the ashram. Taking it all as a sign, Marie was on her way to India for the first time.

Marie met Sri Sai Kaleshwar, and upon first glance at her, the guru said, "The problem with the kind of heartbreak you have is that if you let it heal, it will leave scar tissue on the soul, slowing the soul's journey, so it's better if we just pull it." Not knowing what that meant, and still reeling from sadness, Marie went along with his approach since it sounded like an improvement.

The guru gave her a practice, a mantra to do in the morning and afternoon under a tree. He instructed her to write down things to let go of, and he told her to show up at the fire pit the next night. Like so many of us who have been through a difficult "perfect storm" time, she describes how she was just going through the motions with very little expectation; she followed the instructions.

At the fire pit ceremony, which is called a *fire puja*, Marie felt the divine presence of the teacher as he gave instructions in Telugu to the Brahmin priests conducting the process. Not fully understanding what was going on, Marie nonetheless remained fully present. At the end of the 45-minute ceremony, as Marie stood up, she became aware that her depression was totally gone, and suddenly, she was awash with a deep, heightened sense of peace, unlike anything she had ever felt before. She describes it as "the gift of actual inner silence. Deep inner peace. Total equanimity and oneness."

She says she wasn't looking for a teacher, "but I found him indisputably." Kaleshwar told her, "You have no permission in this lifetime to ever be heartbroken again."

Amazingly, the dear friend, Gary, who originally helped set her on her path to India, is now her deep love and true soul mate. Together, they have opened themselves to the freedom of being seen, to creating something extraordinary together, and to being deeply supportive of each other's chosen paths. Marie says that among Kaleshwar's many teachings that captured her and Gary's commitment and passion are to help "leaders create peace" and that the "real master is in us, waiting to be discovered and put to use serving humanity."

Marie continues to be a sought-after executive leadership consultant and coach. As Managing Partner with the Praemia Group, her clients have included Allstate, Novartis, Reebok, and Whole Foods. She helps executives to develop a deep self-awareness, and to navigate both the business journey of producing results and the change journey of creating a new future.

Although Marie does not usually share her ashram experience with clients, she embodies several of the important leadership lessons she's learned there, such as, "You cannot really lead if you don't know where you are standing, and you can't know where you are standing if you can't access presence at all." She explains that "the truth of that presence and centeredness are as important as having very clear commitments and action plans in place to deliver extraordinary results. You can't do one without the other. You have to engage hearts, not just minds."

How can Marie's experience help us, especially if we are having a dark night of the soul? Marie recommends the following: feel what you are experiencing, be present to what is, use the opportunity to take a deep look at your life direction, accept the support of your beloved friends, consider a drastic change of scenery (even if for a short vacation), be ready for unexpected miracles, be open to a healing coming from something greater than yourself, seize true love when it comes to you, and be ready for an overall up-leveling for the better. Marie has come into her own as the role model she began looking for years ago. She sums it up, sounding triumphant, "If you want to lead, you have to find *you*."

Align Values and Actions:
The Proof in the Pudding

"You are what your deep driving desire is.
As your desire is, so is your will.
As your will is, so is your deed.
As your deed is, so is your destiny."[1]
                        —Brihadaranyaka Upanishad IV. 4.5

A WIND-BLOWN KITE

Early in my struggles with my health challenges, I was walloped with a completely different (*or perhaps totally connected*) gale-force wind that I could not control.

If you had asked me about my deepest, most closely held values back then, I probably would have said something like "being a good person" or "doing my best." That was certainly true, but I found out that even with those beliefs, I was like a lost kite in the wind.

As my adorable oldest daughter, Madeline, went from two to three to four years old, it became clearer with each passing week that she struggled with significant speech, fine motor, gross motor, language, and developmental delays, and an intellectual disability. At these ages, she was unintelligible to everyone except my husband and me (which frustrated her), she was extremely sensitive to sounds (a leaf blower or a loud truck would cause panicked crying), and she sought to calm herself by moving very slowing and fixating on certain things (while she twirled her hair with her head down). For instance, she'd ask me to tell her a favorite Disney plot over and over, and she would ask me 10 or 11 times a day, sometimes two or three times in a row, "Mama, do you love me?"

When my second beautiful daughter, Amelia, was born, two years after Madeline's arrival, her first four months were filled with four to five hours a day of colicky crying. I couldn't make her smile. With all of my other worries, this ongoing wailing heightened my sense of futility. Although I knew colic was temporary (and it was), every day, holding and comforting her, seemed endless. When I asked her pediatrician what was causing this colic, he answered, "Maybe she's not happy."

It's gut-wrenching to see your children suffer in any way, whether it is ongoing or temporary. We set Madeline up with one-to-one physical, speech, and other therapy sessions Monday through Friday, and despite my full-time work schedule, I rearranged client appointments, brought her myself, and sat in on the sessions. I desperately wanted to learn how I could help her. I carried Amelia on my hip whenever I was with her.

My then-husband gradually increased his international work travel schedule (I could hardly blame him), which left me mostly on my own during the week. As I struggled, my "doing my best" and "being a good person" values seemed really flimsy, like a cheap kite. I used those phrases in moments of total frustration, sometimes telling myself, "Sheesh! I am doing my best here!" I didn't quite know how to handle things, except to muscle through one day at a time. I was barely getting by.

THE EMERGENCE OF THE UNIVERSAL
ALIGN VALUES AND ACTIONS SPOKE

I found myself explaining this stressful situation to one of my alternative medicine doctors, who had called me in because my inflammation markers were off the charts. Unexpectedly, she asked me what I felt every morning, the moment I woke up. I honestly answered, "Worry. Dread. Fear." I explained that I never knew what meltdown or "mayday" daycare call or taxing moment lurked around the corner. I told her it seemed like my best wasn't good enough. I remember sobbing and using her whole box of Kleenexes.

She then said something totally unexpected that was life-changing for me. She said, "What if you treated your girls as if they were *goddesses?* What if you woke up and your first thought was that they are *blessings,* gifts, gracing your home with their divine nature? That you get to be in *their* presence?"

In my heart, I knew that essentially, she was right. I had been playing defense every day, on heightened watch, on edge, and something massive needed to shift. In that moment, my *Align Values and Actions* spoke came into being.

Values are the fundamental beliefs, principles, morals, or guideposts that help direct your actions. Since everyone is different, and since everyone resonates with different values, it's important to define this for yourself.

In his closing address to the Global Buddhist Congregation in 2011, His Holiness the Dalai Lama wisely stated, "If you carry out right actions, positive results come."[2] Values provide that groundwork and clear vision for right actions, and I certainly wanted some positive results.

Writer Adam Fridman, in his *Inc.* article "Four Essential Habits to Align Purpose and Values with Actions," says, "The idea that values matter is tied to one of the defining tenets of positive psychology, which is that people seek intrinsic versus extrinsic motivation. They're seeking motivation from within."[3] That is how I felt: I wanted a deep-seated foundation *within* me—something that I had defined, that had meaning for me, and that would give me more positive personal power.

I love the 54 values charted in Tony Jeary's *Success Magazine* online article "Do Your Actions Reflect Your Values?" Sometimes it helps to see the dessert tray rather than come up with the best choice out of thin air, right? Some values listed are creativity, altruism, generosity, power, education, fairness, inner peace, wisdom, travel, solitude, openness, friendship, freedom, faith, joy, efficiency, intimacy, philanthropy, fairness, recognition, productivity, cooperation, and contentment.[4] All of these seem valuable, and they resonate with different people.

When I was sitting in that doctor's office, done with my crying, I realized that my deepest values needed shifting. I pondered the doctor's surprising advice and landed on the word LOVE. What if from now on, my actions were driven by LOVE? What if *LOVE* was my deepest value? What if I woke up with love in my heart and acted with love? In the next month or so, I had a pendant made, 22k gold, inlaid with a single diamond, with the word LOVE stamped on it. I still wear it every single day.

I also thought about the importance of TRUTH, which floated to the surface as an essential value, in the sense of accepting the truth of *what is*. What if I just accepted that things were challenging for specific reasons, what if I was honest with myself about what was happening and the extra efforts it would require, and what if I was good with that?

These two new values brought me out of my self-focused "doing my best" attitude (and really, how would that even be measured?) and grounded me in both an inward- *and* outward-focused strategy. This revamp allowed me to be in service to myself, and in service to others.

It's somewhat embarrassing to admit, but the magnitude of this shift in myself, which actually occurred overnight, had dramatically positive effects in my daughters. I woke the next morning with an authentic, heartfelt openness; greeted each girl sweetly as she woke up; and made them their breakfasts with a softness I hadn't really felt very often. To my immense astonishment, the girls' behavior changed noticeably, even from that first day. Perhaps because Amelia's newborn colic had run its course, or perhaps because that sensitive baby girl had been picking up on my seething panic, her colic stopped *that week*. Madeline's morning meltdowns diminished. She shifted to acting a bit more helpful in getting ready for nursery school, even letting me help her put on her shoes, which had been a struggle up to that point. Within a few weeks, she stopped cowering around loud sounds. Maybe my energy had been loud to her. Ouch.

From then on, each and every time Madeline asked, "Mama, do you love me?" I answered kindly, as if it was the first time I heard it, "I love you so much. You are incredible. I am so lucky to have you." I probably have said those exact words thousands of times over the years.

Watching the two of these girls grow into incredible, unique, genuine loving teenagers has been my life's greatest joy. Madeline relishes being in plays and musicals. Amelia is a happy, peaceful, and thoughtful person who is mature beyond her years. Has it always been calm trade winds? Absolutely not. In fact, the other evening Amelia told me I need to stop worrying so much. Because I am grounded in my values, I listened to that truth, took it in, and responded with a loving smile. I told her I'd keep working on it.

LOVE and TRUTH became my two highest values, and they still are to this day. They put a steel cable on my wind-blown kite.

THE *ALIGN VALUES AND ACTIONS SPOKE* AND WEALTH-BEING

What did vastly improving my *Align Values and Actions* spoke do for me? It moved me from a defensive, reticent role into an empowered leadership role.

On the positive personal outcomes ring of the Wealth-Being Wheel, I experienced alignment, the deep inner peace of knowing that your most deeply held beliefs are being manifested by your actions. There is immense power in doing what you say you are going to do. It was easy for me to judge if I was coming from love in any given situation, because the opposite and my former go-to was fear. This alignment made life exponentially easier, because coming from love *enlivens* you.

As far as positive professional outcomes, my *Align Values and Actions* spoke motivated me at work, and it put a spring in my step. Knowing your values helps you understand your purpose. I had always aimed to bring truth to clients in my wealth management business. Transparency had always been paramount and a competitive advantage, but defining truth as a deeply held value during this time of my life helped me express it more prominently, which I categorize under communication mastery. *Love* is not really a value word people use aloud in my line of work, but I would say that from a place of respect for each client, a deep caring, I was able to best be of service, which on the Wealth-Being Wheel is expressed as impeccable service.

Are you ready to experience this game-changing spoke? Let's go.

CUSTOMIZING THE *ALIGN VALUES AND ACTIONS* SPOKE FOR YOU

1. Identify two to five values that are important to YOU. Don't worry about anyone else. If you respect the values you grew up with, keep those. If you don't, consider new ones. What resonates for you as a personal foundation, or a guiding light, so to speak?

2. Make a few notes next to each value to indicate why they are important to you. For instance, if you write *loyalty* as a value, then define what that means to you, and maybe even write a great example of how you express it in your life. You want to lock that value into your awareness.

3. Muse a bit on how each of these values might help you in a difficult situation. Sometimes you can take a current issue and look at it through the lens of that defined value. For example, if your value is respect, consider how you might handle that difficult negotiation at work, the one that broke down last week. This is a helpful way of making aligned decisions that move you forward in ways that feel good to you.

4. Think of your personal and professional values, and see if there are any on your list that authentically qualify as both. That makes things very clear and easy. In fact, I think it is the ideal.

If you can apply your values to both work and home, then they follow you everywhere you go.

5. Pretend you are cleaning your garage, only let's think of that action as a symbol of your life. Is there anything in your "garage" that doesn't fit with your values? When I started to live consciously by my values, it made it easier to get rid of activities, groups, appointments—and yes, even people—who didn't resonate with my values. It made it so much easier to define boundaries once I knew what *I* stood for.

6. If you have no clue how to figure out what your values are, list the things you enjoy doing, and you can discover the underlying value from there. For instance, say you love seeing live music. Think about what it is that you value so much—tease it apart. Is it creativity that you value? Is it the excellence of the performers? That is a good way to get to the core value.

7. Start aligning your stated values with your actions. Look forward to peace, contentment, and power.

INCREDIBLE WELL-BEING CUSTOMIZATIONS FROM AN EXCEPTIONAL EXECUTIVE

Steven Rice, Chief Human Resources Officer, Bill & Melinda Gates Foundation

Steven Rice completed 50 roundtrip flights between San Francisco and Seattle last year, and to say the least, the airport gate agents know him by name. Flying into Seattle, he says he always loves the view of the Space Needle and the Bill & Melinda Gates Foundation (which he calls "The Foundation"), especially on a rare sunny day. These frequent plane flights give him plenty of time to ask himself a question he has been considering for years: "Am I living an intentional life?" His consistent answer these days is *undoubtedly yes*. He says that the more mature he becomes, "the more clarity I get."

Steven Rice is Chief Human Resources Officer for the Bill & Melinda Gates Foundation, the world's largest philanthropic organization, which is based in Seattle. Recruited in 2015, Steven oversees the global HR functions of talent, leadership, and organizational culture and organizational alignment for more than 1,500 employees worldwide. He raves that "I get to work with and meet some of the brightest individuals on the planet in this role." One of his many aims? "To make this feel like a family."

In 2017, the foundation released to the public a forward-thinking educational whitepaper that Steven coauthored, entitled "Innovative Practices for Leading Culture."[5] With a generosity of spirit characteristic of Steven, it lays out challenges and puts forth strategies around how everyone as individuals, and also as aligned teams, can do their best work, and thus, have maximal organizational impact.

This whitepaper shares the Gates Foundation workforce commitments, or values, dubbed the "Four Agreements: How We Treat Each Other," which include *Show Respect* (Inclusion, Kindness, Humility), *Offer Trust* (Risk Taking, Collaboration, Empowerment), *Be Transparent* (Clarity, Communications), and *Create Energy* (Engagement, Pursuit of Becoming our Best Self).[6] Although these four distinct goals are entirely related to the foundation, they also provide an innovative and succinct framework to illuminate how Steven personally lives his life.

In the *Show Respect* category, to say that Steven cares about people is an understatement. He explains that his entire 30 years in human resource leadership has been fueled by "a deep love for fostering the maximum employee potential within each organization I have served." Before joining the Gates Foundation, Steven was Executive Vice President of Human Resources at technology network provider Juniper Networks, where, as the top HR executive, he oversaw a workforce of more than 9,000 employees in more than 70 countries. Steven was a hugely respected leader there, and former colleagues still express gratitude about his impact on them. Before Juniper Networks, he worked at

Hewlett-Packard for 25 years, rising from working in entry-position quality control while he finished his education to being responsible for the
global delivery of HR for 2,000 people in 172 countries. He never lost his
humility, and he relates with deep respect to colleagues at all levels. He
says that in every role he has had, his intent is "to see how I can serve."

Also in the *Show Respect* area, Steven's deep-seated belief, echoed
by the Gates Foundation's overarching guiding light, is that "all lives
have equal value."[7] The son of parents who lived through the Depression, Steven learned early on from their leadership to work hard, to venture out, and to try to help the community at large. While at Juniper
Networks, he chaired the Juniper Networks Foundation Fund, which
supports educating K–12 students in STEM (Science, Technology, Engineering, and Math), bringing technology to underserved communities,
and stopping human trafficking. In 2013, Steven was nominated for
the Business Leader's Award to Fight Human Trafficking, a joint effort
between End Human Trafficking Now and the United Nations. It matters to Steven that he makes a difference.

At the Gates Foundation, he finds himself in perfect alignment with
initiatives for global health, global development, US high school and
post-secondary education, and helping vulnerable communities.

In the *Offer Trust* value set, it's worth mentioning his consciousness
of values, his ability to verbalize them, and his corresponding actions.
He says, "My personal power comes from standing clearly. I am coura-
geous, clear, deliberate, and authentic, and that all enhances leadership capability."

In the *Be Transparent* category, he says he is interested "in the
bridge between one's passion and the mission of the organization.
How does one's personal goals get met at work?" He's interested in
the design of work, and inclusion, such as how to tap into the intellectual capital and valuable contribution of employees in emerging
markets. He's at the forefront of asking questions, be it for his organization or publicly via the *Harvard Business Review,* stretching to the next
level, and thus, he is one of the most prominent leadership voices in HR
worldwide.

In the *Create Energy* category, Steven and his partner and highly accomplished husband of 35 years, Gary, have worked out an enlivening dual-city life that they consistently communicate about. Because their main home base is in the San Francisco enclave of Hillsborough, and because Gary's company is based in San Francisco and Steven's usual workweek is in Seattle (or, if traveling, he could be in Beijing, London, or elsewhere around the world), needless to say they are often separated during the week. They have agreed to regroup every 12 months to review if this "divide-and-conquer" career situation is working for them. Steven says, in a positive way, that "life is a constant number of compromises." So far so good.

Steven, who has an easy laugh and a frequent smile, says, "My relationship is part of my well-being," and therefore it is a value he holds dear. When he and Gary are together, their ventures center around walking their beloved soft-coated Wheaten terrier, Ms. Penny, and exploring creativity. Steven says he is "curious about art," and because they collect art and "love art for different reasons," he and Gary can be found together at Art Basel Munich and at Art Basel Miami: high-profile, live art show events featuring the masters of modern and contemporary art. Lovers of fashion, they attended Men's Fashion Week in Milan as private guests of the Prada store in Beverly Hills (which Steven refers to as the "Mother Ship"), and he says it is so rewarding "to have shared passions."

Steven concludes, "I believe in destiny." It's obvious that the alignment of his most deeply held values and actions, the coordination of what he says and what he does, have him headed toward a continued life of impact.

Speak Your Truth:
Just Deliver It with Grace

"Speaking your truth is the most powerful tool we all have."[1]

—Oprah Winfrey, 2018 Golden Globes

FEAR OF WAVES

When I was in my early twenties, I almost drowned in the ocean off the coast of San Diego. Having grown up in the midst of cornfields, I had very little exposure to the ocean, so when I was newly situated in California, it was an opportunity to try something new. My boyfriend at the time, who was teaching windsurfing at the Mission Bay Aquatic Center, was an absolute natural in the ocean. On a beautiful Saturday morning, he outfitted us with shortie wetsuits and boogie boards, gave me some basic instructions, and added some lighthearted encouragement. Then we jumped into the waves together.

The power of the water and waves overwhelmed, knocked, tossed, and unexpectedly disoriented me. In what seemed like only a few minutes, a riptide pulled me way out. Suddenly, the sounds of beach laughter were replaced with absolute, eerie silence.

I was completely alone and surrounded by such huge swells on all sides of me that I couldn't even see which way the shore was. Although a decent swimmer, I had no idea which way to swim, so I started treading water. Without a life jacket, and somehow without my boogie board, I absolutely panicked, my heart crushing in fear that I might die out there.

I bobbed out there alone, time moving painfully slow, with my senses as sharp as a razor, and with my arms and legs exhausted and burning to stay afloat. In one of the most unexpected moments of my entire life, from *underneath* the water, a black-haired boy, about eight years old, bobbed up like a cork and appeared next to me, bare-chested, with no wetsuit (which is odd in Pacific Ocean water that cold). In his right hand, he brought forth my boogie board. He simply said, "Here you go!" and he gave it to me. And then, I swear to God, he vanished. He didn't swim away, he just vanished into thin air. To this day I believe he was an angel that saved my life.

That day also imprinted in me a deep fear for the ocean, and especially waves.

Fast forward to 13 years later, when I was living in the Bay Area. My husband (a different but similarly adventurous man) decided to take up sailing on the San Francisco Bay, one of the most technically difficult places in the world to sail because of the winds, which can be serene one hour and screaming at gale force the next. As the (very true) saying goes, "If you can sail in San Francisco, you can sail anywhere in the world."[2]

After he literally sailed through his beginning to advanced courses, he encouraged *me* to take up sailing too. He wanted us to have something new to do together, and as any new parents know, you are grasping for non-baby-related things at that point in your life.

Now I need to pause here to admit that although he had heard my ocean story, I had diminished the harrowing aspect. He assumed that the way I tiptoed away from the surf as we walked on the beach was more of a cute quirk.

I also need to admit that I hadn't thoroughly shared the excruciating physical pain I was in. Although he knew my body pain was generally high, I kept the daily "rheumatoid arthritis report" out of our conversations (I mean, talk about a romance killer right there!). I really didn't want to be a disabled wife. However, because I hardly ever mentioned my pain, it wasn't top of mind for him, and he optimistically thought I could sail.

To my shock, I opened my birthday gift from him that year: a voucher for a US Sailing Basic Keelboat Certification Course on the San Francisco Bay, starting the following weekend. I shoved down my panic and pretended to be excited.

During the next two terrorizing weekends of whitecaps, brutally cold February rain, howling winds, the 24-foot sailboat heeling over at a terrifying 45-degree angle, and man overboard protocol and testing, I somehow endured and kept my shivering chin up.

Totally ungrounded on the boat, I clung to the side lines and marveled at the ease of our salty, weathered teacher, who would perch on the metal railing, practically touching the waves crashing along his back, and telling tall sailing stories, each ending with "and then she went down like a greased refrigerator!"

Because—if anything—I am an overachiever, to my husband's immense delight, I passed the certification test with flying colors.

From then on, whenever he invited me to go sailing I smiled and agreed, because I wanted him to think I was that fun, up-for-anything girl he fell in love with. However, out on the open water, my swallowed truths—both my ongoing fear of the waves and my excruciating physical pain—bubbled up to the surface and ruined our time together. These hidden truths, wouldn't you know, *actually seemed to attract* the very worst in San Francisco Bay foul weather, brutal wind, and ridiculous sailboat malfunctions.

To make things worse, I felt deeply resentful that I was *pretending* to be a good sport for his benefit (I mean, he didn't know the extent of my *sacrifice!*), but underneath that, I was really just mad at myself for not speaking my truth. Who did I think I was fooling? He had wanted me to be there with him and to be happy, but it was the last place I wanted to be. Do you see the disaster?

STEPPING INTO THE *SPEAK YOUR TRUTH* SPOKE

I learned that the biggest risk of not speaking your truth is that people, many of whom are closest to you, don't know who you *really* are. My sailing story, only a small glimpse, pointed to a much bigger truth. At times, I had to admit, I was being the person I thought others *wanted* me to be, rather than being myself.

From an early age, I often heard family members declare, "If you don't have anything nice to say, don't say it." As a survival mechanism, I learned to not ruffle feathers, to keep quiet, to "be good." However, as an adult, absent any pending punishment, it morphed into a situation in which I frequently maintained a "Miss Cheerful" veneer even when I was suffering inside.

What I learned is that if you keep your truth inside, you ultimately isolate yourself. You distance yourself from key support systems. You become one of the very few people who really knows the authentic *you*. That is stressful to balance all by your lonesome, and it takes a huge toll on well-being.

I learned my lesson from that sailing experience, owned my fault in the issue, and decided that I would begin to embrace my truth. I decided to start speaking my truth in small ways. For instance, if someone asked me how I was, such a typical question, I practiced being honest. I'd say, "Ugh! Not the easiest morning!" and I was shocked at how often that authenticity opened *them* up. They'd respond with something like "I feel the same way!" and we were off to the races with something much more real.

I moved up from there, and since how I really felt about sailing was so transparently obvious, I told my husband. He was fine with it and enlisted a diehard sailing buddy, who ended up completing many long sails with him (and without me, thank God).

When you start to speak your truth, especially about something hard to say, you will know it was the right thing to do if you immediately feel relief. If you immediately feel dread, like "Gosh, I shouldn't have said that," then it may have been your chosen words or tone or timing. You'll get better.

I believe it's important to commit to speaking your truth with grace. I journal a lot before speaking heavier truths. I really think through my words, looking at all angles, even writing out scripts (no kidding) as a practice for what I am about to say. When you make a committed shift like this, it pays to be lovingly conscious, and to consider the potential effect on your audience.

As spiritual teacher Iyanla Vanzant wisely notes, "In speaking the truth of your experience to another, it will serve you well to realize that how they choose to respond is not your responsibility."[3] I agree in theory, but nevertheless, I was terrified about possible repercussions. Admittedly, it was my biggest hurdle. Would the people I was being honest with accept me? What would the fallout be? I was worried I would lose friends, distance family members, and rattle work colleagues.

Little by little, I realized how freeing it was to speak my truth. Did I lose some people who were formerly close to me? Absolutely. Did some really not like this new truth-teller? Certainly. Do I think that the fallout was for the best? Absolutely. Did I find new, more authentic connections? No question. Did I ever regret embracing this spoke like my new best friend? Not once.

THE *SPEAK YOUR TRUTH* SPOKE AND WEALTH-BEING

This *Speak Your Truth* spoke is a commitment to loving yourself wholly and completely enough to communicate who you are and what you think.

As far as positive personal outcomes, just to give you a sense of its meaning to me, its profound effect on my well-being, I have only one tattoo on my body (on my right shoulder). In Sanskrit, it says "Sat Nam," which translates to "my name is truth," "truth is my identity," and also "everlasting truth." It's that important to me. Owning my truth points to the "know" part of the Wealth-Being Wheel, which means a deep inner knowing of my own convictions. It also points to my confidence in sharing them.

If your loved ones care about you, which they do, then they deeply appreciate knowing what you think. This improved all of my relationships.

As far as positive professional outcomes on the Wealth-Being Wheel, my *Speak Your Truth* spoke leads me straight to communication mastery, which resides in the art of flawlessly saying what you mean to say, with the emotional intelligence to present your truth with the finesse and power to get your point across with that particular person. Because I am in a sales position, how I present my truthful ideas for serving a client is critical, and success in this area improves my bottom line and further points to financial freedom and maximum profitability.

Are you ready to open up your truth channels and experience this critical spoke? Here we go!

CUSTOMIZING THE *SPEAK YOUR TRUTH* SPOKE FOR YOU

1. To help you get to the heart of the real you, the truth of what you *really* think, I created a helpful practice. When you have a bit of uninterrupted time, at the top of a blank piece of paper write "What is true is that…" Then write as many things as you can think of, from the mundane to the monumental. During my healing, I did this practice over and over to see what I *really* thought. It can be astonishing to discover what comes out when you don't censor yourself.

2. Is there something on that list or something you just know that really needs to be shared? Start planning for it to emerge into that important conversation you need to have.

3. I want to share a helpful trick for getting out a truth that is a criticism, and I call this personal strategy the "criticism sandwich." It helps the listener stomach your critique. You

start with a genuine compliment (e.g., "Our relationship means the world to me") and then the criticism from your point of view (e.g., "and so I want to share that your 14-hour work days have us all missing you") and then the compliment (e.g., "You mean so much to us"). See how that works? Is there a way that you could use that to soften the delivery of an important truth?

INCREDIBLE WELL-BEING CUSTOMIZATIONS FROM AN EXCEPTIONAL EXECUTIVE

Judy Belk, President and CEO, The California Wellness Foundation

Judy Belk has had a stressful year. She explains, "I lost three really important people in my life. My grandmother used to say that people always die in threes, and I thought, here you go."

As a go-to strategy for dealing with this type of toll-taking stress, Judy turns to her writing. For more than 30 years, the underlying power source of Judy's career trajectory has been her consistently clear voice and her communication talent, which she finds most easily accessed through her craft of writing. To access her deepest truths, she says, "I have to write about it to work through it."

In a world where many curate a perfect picture of their lives on social media, Judy says she feels that dealing successfully with grief and tragedy is "an important part of awareness" that has given her "a lens in terms of viewing things." Having experienced sexual abuse as a child, and later, going through the heartbreaking loss of her older sister, Vickie, who was murdered by gun violence at age 28, Judy garnered not only an appreciation for therapy ("It was critical in a very positive way") but also a deep respect for the power that comes with being real. Judy, who is African American, uses her ability to access the truth of situations to garner power beyond herself and to speak out as a fearless voice in conversations around race, family, community, and social change.

Judy Belk is President and CEO of The California Wellness Foundation (Cal Wellness), a private $1 billion-plus foundation that focuses on improving the quality of health, employment, and safety of underserved people in the state. The foundation has a long history of taking on the most challenging issues of our time, such as gun violence prevention and access to health care.

Before Cal Wellness, she spent 12 years as Senior Vice President of Rockefeller Philanthropy Advisors, which she helped build into one of the world's largest independent nonprofit advisory firms, advising on more than $300 million annually in 30 countries. Before that, she did a decade-long corporate stint as VP of Global Affairs at Levi Strauss & Co, with a worldwide staff, and as a direct report to the CEO. She led efforts in the company's fight against AIDS, women's economic development, and a national anti-racism initiative, and the company was honored with President Bill Clinton's first Ron Brown Award for Corporate Leadership. Her past board appointments include The Berkeley Repertory Theater, the Ms. Foundation for Women, and the American Civil Liberties Union of Northern California, and each offers direct insight into what she cares about.

Interestingly, as much as she is in the public eye with her work, she found her unique voice and confidence in her truth during an awarded residency at a quiet, remote women writer's retreat called Hedgebrook, which is on Whidbey Island in Washington. (Gloria Steinem is a past alum.) At Hedgebrook, she had extra time to think because she had just left Levi Strauss. Secluded with just a handful of other famous and emerging writers, she cemented her vision for using her truth to help others. She says that the transformative weeks "changed my life."

Back home in Los Angeles today, Judy maintains that Hedgebrook spirit with a unique commitment to getting her voice heard, and she attains the essential comradery by participating in a writing group. Writing takes practice, and she's committed to honing her skills. Every other

Saturday, she drives from Hollywood to Santa Monica (and if you have experienced L.A. traffic, then you will sense the commitment here) to sit with five other writers at their writing coach's home. Some are working on memoirs and some on sci-fi; Judy is working on personal essays.

In her writing, Judy uses her immensely powerful platform and well-known talent for brilliant expression to execute her top core value, which is "the greater common good." Her essays have been featured in USA Today, The New York Times, The Los Angeles Times, The Washington Post, National Public Radio, The Wall St. Journal, and many other publications.

For instance, in an essay titled "Memories of a Thirsty Childhood,"[4] Judy sheds light on current day water poverty, the desperate need for impoverished people to access clean water; she poignantly reveals that through age 12, although she lived only 10 miles from the White House in Alexandria, Virginia, in her black community, her family didn't have running water or indoor plumbing. She furthers the message that access to clean water is a human right.

In an op-ed spotlighting the experience of racism[5] and being a black man in America, Judy talks about her husband, a physician, and the story of her then 23-year-old son (who now has a PhD in History) and his strategies to make others on BART, the subway system in the Bay Area, comfortable in his, a black man's, presence.

In stories about Vickie, her beloved sister who died just two weeks after being Judy's maid of honor, she humanizes the devastating effect of gun violence. Between Judy's voice and the California Wellness Foundation's stance, gun violence, like all community violence, is presented as a public health issue.

Her ability to speak her truth has inspired her grown children as well. After four years of teaching kindergarten, including a stint for Teach for America, her daughter wants to make a difference with a career in public service; she just earned a Masters in Educational Policy at Harvard University.

Judy manages to keep things down to earth while being one of the only African American women running a foundation of this size. Every day when she arrives at work, she makes the rounds, speaking to each of her staff, who, she proudly declares, are a very diverse group. If she needs some personal support, she calls on her "kitchen cabinet" of women friends she has known for decades, and whom she treasures for knowing her beyond her title. Judy knows these women can be counted on to give her a swift kick to do things that frighten her, like convincing her to apply for her current CEO position.

She explains, "There's a lot of flattery that comes your way when you're in a position of power, influence, and money. If I let it, it could change me in ways that wouldn't be good for me or my work. But if I use that influence wisely, I could marshal it to open closed doors, shine a spotlight on unmet needs, and speak out on issues that might otherwise go unheard."

In 2013, this powerhouse—who used to carry buckets of water for her family's needs, who read second-hand Nancy Drew novels from the white family her grandmother worked for, and who graduated from Northwestern University—was inducted into the Alexandria African American Hall of Fame in recognition of her writing and commitment to social change.

Judy says that her journey to "where I can be who I am and where I can bring those values together" has been a critical, conscious choice all along. She takes speaking your truth to a whole new level, and says, "I tell folks that *you take who you are with you through life.*" And we are certainly all the better for being invited to journey with her.

Hone Your Focus:
Zoning in like a Laser

"Focus on the possibilities for success, not the
potential for failure."[1]

—Napoleon Hill

FEAR LOOPS

When I started my career in financial services and learned about the low salary the first few years in the intense training program (you really have to put in your dues), I remember my husband saying, "There's no one as motivated as you, Megan. You will succeed." And I did. We both knew that as far as my career, I had the gift of complete focus. Of the 100 trainees in my training program who started the exact day I did, only two of us are left.

Right out of the gate, I had a written, detailed business plan about how I really wanted to help people *and* succeed, and I shared that business plan with every senior advisor in my office on the East Bay and also in San Francisco. Not only did I become known as a go-getter, but also these senior leaders helped me hone my focus further, suggesting brilliant improvements. I was so focused on success that the firm had me record an audio lecture on the importance of business planning, and it is still required learning for all new trainees, firm-wide, 20 years later.

That was all well and good, but when I was diagnosed with my first disease, the rheumatoid arthritis, I was thrown *way* off my focus game. As you know, I immediately began creating a business type of plan to heal myself, which is the Well-Being Wheel, because having a written plan for getting better made perfect sense to me. During my healing journey with the Wheel, however, I discovered something shocking.

I didn't realize how much I was focusing on the *negative* when it came to my health, like a moth careening to the light. It was a *situational* focus issue, and something I needed to get control of.

The intense pain from the rheumatoid arthritis, which felt like crushed glass embedded in my wrists and nails driving through my feet, hijacked my attention. *Every time I walked* I noticed that pain (Ow!), which led to a quick moment of despair (Ugh!), which led to an instant feeling of distress (What if this doesn't go away?), which led to more pain and, you guessed it, despair and stress. I found myself stuck in a self-inflicted, negatively focused loop: I couldn't stop thinking about the pain.

When I was later diagnosed with chronic kidney disease (FSGS), there was no physical pain, but as the doctors tried to stop my kidneys from failing, which was a much more health-threatening situation than the rheumatoid arthritis, I struggled with deep-seated fear. This disease upped the ante on my overall desperation. I had two diseases now (gulp). My mind frequently ran away in a loop of fear (What if I end up on dialysis?) to despair to distress and, you guessed it, more fear.

When I was diagnosed with kidney cancer after that, by far the biggest challenge related to mind control, I faced a horrifying disease that, in a more runaway form, could actually kill me. This was an even more intense fear-despair-stress-fear loop. I worried that if I didn't solve this threefold disease crisis, I would leave my daughters, 12 and 14 at the time, motherless.

I had an absolute sense that I needed to get control of my mind. It wasn't an overall depression; it was how I was focusing on these situations specifically. For a high achiever like myself, it's a tough nut to crack: the concept that you might be hurting yourself by your negatively focused thoughts. I thought I was better than that, but there I was, obsessing with fear.

ZONING IN ON THE *HONE YOUR FOCUS* SPOKE

You may have heard the idea that what we resist seems to come at us in spades. It means that what you *don't* want gains an energy that becomes more powerful. It's true! Anyone who has had a cascading bad day knows this.

As I created this spoke, I became a huge fan of *The Law of Attraction*,[2] an important and brilliant book by Esther and Jerry Hicks, which was making the rounds at about the same time as the runaway bestselling 2006 film and book *The Secret*,[3] by Rhonda Byrne. In the former, the authors lay out the second law of attraction, which hit me like a ton of bricks: "That which I give thought to and that which I believe or expect—*is*."[4] Every time I read that now, I reread it and emphasize the *is*. I realized that I was giving energy and thought to what I *didn't* want. I was attracting the negative by giving it top priority. No wonder I wasn't healed yet! I was subconsciously sabotaging myself.

Many of us have unhealthy focus patterns in our own lives—patterns that may be diminishing our power. Most of us have seen this law of attraction in action. For instance, we're nervous before our speech that the AV equipment might not work properly with our laptop, and bam, there's a technology issue.

This *Hone Your Focus* spoke came into being when I set about changing my fear-based focus into an empowering focus. Because I am efficient and didn't have any time to lose, I decided to do three things: to take note of my consistently occurring dread-based thoughts, to stop them at the pass, and to start telling myself the exact opposite.

For instance, whenever I noticed myself thinking, "What if my cancer comes back?" I instantly acknowledged it ("There you are again!"), stopped it, and replaced it with "I am healed and getting better every day." Then I added, "Vibrant health is my path."

Another frequent downer was "What if I need a kidney transplant someday?" However, I noticed it, stopped it ("Enough already!"), and replaced it with "My kidneys are stable, and everything is going to be just fine."

Let me note here that saying these things (often out loud) in the middle of a serious health crisis seemed ridiculous at best and utter denial at worst. I didn't care. What I did realize is that *thinking the better thought* made me feel better. I then took the new thoughts a step further, visualizing my kidneys filtering my blood beautifully, humming along. I imagined the little leftover cancer cells getting crushed by my powerful immune system. It was kind of fun! Certainly better than worrying.

Let me also say that shifting your mind away from legitimate fear is one of the hardest things in the world to do. To stop thinking about cancer when I had it was one of the hardest challenges I have *ever* faced, bar none. For others to stop thinking about their particular elephant in the room is similarly, monumentally difficult.

Hone Your Focus became a game-changer in my well-being strategy. You cannot discount the healing power of this type of massive energy shift. There is a ton of research on the power of visualization and using mental imagery, in conjunction with positive affirmations. Everyone from Olympic athletes to CEOs uses these tools to enhance the likelihood of a more positive future outcome.

Jennice Vilhauer, PhD, in her *Psychology Today* article "3 Effective Visualization Techniques to Change Your Life," notes that you can increase your chances of success by learning "to use visualization to actively create future simulations that can help you improve goals that you set for yourself."[5] She says that adding as much detail and emotional intensity as you can helps "so that you begin to feel the experience of it, as if it were real."[6] You are basically training your mind into a new reality. I did exactly that. I worked a lot on imagining the positive outcome I wanted and feeling that it was indeed true.

Interestingly, it all *did* become true, and I am deeply grateful.

THE *HONE YOUR FOCUS* SPOKE AND WEALTH-BEING

This *Hone Your Focus* spoke was the hardest for me to master, but it is one of the most powerful aids to move you toward well-being and success.

As far as positive personal outcomes on the Wealth-Being Wheel, I experienced the motivating outcome of drive, that single focus toward your supreme goal. I had experienced it all along with my career, but now I applied it to my health. Immediately, it affected my mood, and instead of arriving at a location having worried uncontrollably for 30 minutes, I arrived pumped up, excited, and inspired. I felt groundedness, a deep confidence in myself and my path.

I learned, importantly, that FEAR and HOPE cannot exist at the same time. Try it. You cannot hold both feelings simultaneously at once. Fear tears down but hope builds. I also have heard it said about fear and love that we have the power to choose, and therefore we have the power to manifest whichever we focus on. Give me the hope and love, please.

As far as positive professional outcomes on the Wealth-Being Wheel, my *Hone Your Focus* spoke landed on peak performance, because instead of wasting energy in my free time imagining the worst scenario, I had more time to conjure the best case and produce a superior result. As I mentioned, I had already mastered *Hone Your Focus* as far as my career, but with the coordination of the *Hone Your Focus* spoke in my personal life with relation to my health, it was as if this talent overall was boosted even further. Because I began doing exponentially better at work, I would also add that another result was market superiority. No longer was I focused at work but ungrounded in my personal life. I practiced the techniques consistently, so the energy was productively coordinated and overall amplified.

To me now, it's a luxury to focus on the immense turn that my life has taken for the better and the extraordinary, beautiful reality I live.

Are you ready to focus in on this critical spoke? Let's do it!

CUSTOMIZING THE *HONE YOUR FOCUS* SPOKE FOR YOU

1. Let's just dive right in. What do you fear the most? Do you play horrible, undesirable future scenarios in your mind? You are not alone. Write as many fears as you can on a piece of paper. Don't censor yourself.
2. Now be honest: how much do you focus on these items? Next to each item note how often you think this thought. This can be an enlightening exercise. We need to help you stop doing this.
3. Now think of the exact opposite of each fear, and write it next to that. In fact, go ahead and draw a line through the fear (enough of that harmful garbage) and then write the better thought. For example, if you write "I hope I don't screw up in that important meeting," draw a line through it and replace it with "I am amazing and successful in meetings."
4. Interested in reading more about the law of attraction and your power to manifest what you *do* want? I suggest reading *The Law of Attraction: The Basics on the Teaching of Abraham*[7] and *The Vortex: Where the Law of Attraction Assembles All Cooperative Relationships*,[8] both by Esther and Jerry Hicks. I also love *The Secret*,[9] both the book and documentary, by Rhonda Byrnes.
5. Another absolutely ground-breaking, bestselling book in this arena is *The Biology of Belief: Unleashing the Power of Consciousness, Matter & Miracles*[10] by Bruce H. Lipton, PhD. Both Dr. Lipton and the book are fascinating, and they will forever change the way you think about the way you think.
6. If you suffer from a health issue like I did and are interested in upping your guided-imagery game, I recommend Martin L. Rossman, MD's well-respected audio set *Guided Imagery for Self-Healing*,[11] which I used during my journey.

INCREDIBLE WELL-BEING CUSTOMIZATIONS FROM AN EXCEPTIONAL EXECUTIVE

Robyn Denholm, Chairman of the Board, Tesla Motors, Inc., and Chief Financial Officer and Head of Strategy, Telstra

When Robyn Denholm was young, growing up in the southwestern suburbs of Sydney, Australia, she became a "car enthusiast" by working at her family's service station, helping to pump gas, repair cars, and complete bookwork. A natural at numbers, she took it a step further and became captivated by the power of understanding financials and their potential effect on business strategy, an early-adopted focus that would guide her entire professional career to come.

After spending five years in accounting at Arthur Andersen LLP, she spent seven years at Toyota Motor Corporation Australia, eventually rising to National Manager of Finance. Denholm went on to rise through the financial ranks to eventually head corporate strategic planning for Sun Microsystems, and then, for the following nine years, she acted as Chief Financial and Operations Officer at Juniper Networks. Robyn and her financial leadership are credited for Juniper's great increase in revenue between 2014 and 2016. In early 2017, lured back to her native Australia by a company with five times the revenue and three times the number of employees, Robyn assumed the CFO and Head of Strategy roles at Telstra, Australia's leading telecom and tech company.

Robyn has an easy laugh and a casual manner, and she mentions, delighted by the memory, that in 2014, when she was asked to be on Tesla Motors' board of directors, their first appointed woman since becoming public, she, being the car enthusiast, already had a *Model S* on order. With her deep experience in finance, she heads the board's audit committee. In November 2018, in her most high-profile, most highly publicized appointment yet, Robyn was named Chairman of the Board of Tesla Motors, Inc., succeeding billionaire founder Elon Musk, who remains CEO.

While it would be easy to assume that such a flawless advance—such success in the execution of her dual finance/strategy focus—is a self-propelled achievement, Robyn is quick to correct that notion. Another significant focus of her life has been the importance of mentorship. She explains that she looks up to "as much the people I work for as the people I work with."

At Toyota Australia, in her mid-twenties to early thirties, she met a life-changing mentor, the Chief Financial Officer, a fabulous visionary leader whom she describes as "completely ahead of his time." Instead of having traditional direct reports, he trained her and a cohort of peers in all aspects of his role, and amazingly, they all went on to become successful, next-generation CFOs and senior executives. She says he went beyond encouragement to "supporting you in taking that step beyond where you were. He was really capable of that. He pushed you and believed you could do it."

She can tick off dozens of valued leaders and friends along the way who have mentored her over the years, including Scott Kriens, the 12-year CEO and chairman of the board of Juniper Networks, whom she describes as "a fantastic leader. I learned a tremendous amount from him about working with investors, being a great CFO, about leadership, and about life." She greatly values Kevin Johnson, one of Kriens' CEO successors at Juniper, now the CEO of Starbucks. As a fellow woman executive, she treasures Cathy Benko, Vice Chairman and Managing Principal of Deloitte, who taught her about resilience. She's grateful for Deborah Chase Hopkins, former CFO at Boeing, and former Citigroup's Chief Information Officer and former CEO of Citi Ventures, who connected to Robyn through a work relationship and has been a valued mentor to her in the Bay Area. All of these mentors continue to offer encouragement and truly have her back.

In return, Robyn's focus on the importance of mentorship inspires her to mentor others, to take them under her experienced wing. She has her own cadre of mentees, to whom she imparts what it means to be a C-suite executive in what she describes as "a whole new playing field."

Foundationally, she believes that as a leader, her own authenticity is key. She mentions that she models "having one integrated life. What I do at work and what I do at home is *one life* as opposed to two separate lives. It's authentic because you are one person and you cannot be two people. I have seen it cause burnout. The places where I've thrived from a work perspective are those where I could be my authentic self."

She tweaked this focus on authenticity at Sun Microsystems, and then at Juniper Networks, where one of the company core values is "Champion Authenticity," and where, with the many different streams reporting to her, she soared. At Telstra, she also fit right in, and she acknowledges that "part of the Australian psyche is to be authentic at work."

In a giant break from traditional CFO expectations, and from her own well-known diligent work pattern, she trained her entire staff at Juniper Networks so that she could take a full month off for an extremely special occasion: her honeymoon with her longtime partner, and now husband, David. This was the longest period of time she's ever taken off while working, so she met with the teams beforehand and handed over much of the day-to-day responsibility. Looking back, she says, "They really rose to the occasion over the whole period." Not only did her mentees get a chance to shine, to handle issues in real time using their own acumen, but also they more than met her expectations, and she says, "The place was fantastic when I got back."

As a leader and mentor, one of the most valuable attributes she models is intense curiosity, and she says that "the ability to acknowledge that you don't know something is important and different than twenty years ago. Talking to the team, learning from the team, being able to be real about how I may not know something (although I do know enough to be dangerous), and to have them able to teach me has opened the team to having that sort of relationship as opposed to some sort of control environment." She adds, "You have to learn to be effective and be effective to learn. I have done that well."

She also models that a C-suite executive needs to be front and center, not only number-focused as in days of old, but also a keeper and driver of company culture, a proponent on diversity of thought (a topic she often speaks about publicly), and, of course, highly aware of company strategy, of driving the business toward desired outcomes.

Because of her focus talent, Robyn remains one of the most powerful women—and one of the most influential people—in the corporate world. Her brilliance at finance and business strategy, her appreciation for being mentored, her commitment to mentoring, and even her penchant for cars has brought her to this pinnacle, which offers a completely new, unique view. With her easy manner and quick laugh, Robyn, from where she stands, invites us to trail blaze alongside her.

Master a Positive Attitude: Here Comes the Sun

"We wait, starving for moments of high magic to inspire us, but life is a banquet of common enchantment waiting for our alchemists' eyes to notice."[1]

—Jacob Nordby

A SOFT PITCH

As a child, I studied my grandmother, whom our whole family lovingly called Birdie, with immense admiration. She unexpectedly had been widowed at 58 years old, but even on her own, and perhaps more so because of it, her life continued to expand. As I went through middle school, high school, and college, I often visited her for spring break at her art-filled, bungalow-style house in Tucson all on my own, which was my absolute favorite thing to do. Each time, I marveled at her judgment-free encouragement, her insatiable curiosity, her endless interests, and her boundless positivity.

Whatever I was up to, she thought it was great. Whether I was making turquoise necklaces or studying Wordsworth in the Lake District of England or collecting Tibetan singing bowls, she wanted to hear all about it. Her complete lack of judgment about what I was doing—and more surprising, what I was thinking—drew me to her. I had never met anyone so utterly accepting, so filled with love, so open and free.

We'd sit out at night on lounge chairs on her patio by her pool, float a few candles in the water, and look at the stars together. As a hobby, she had been a senior navigator for the United States Power Squadrons, helping grade celestial navigation exams, and she'd point out constellations I could barely see.

During the day, we'd search for loose, naturally occurring garnets in the desert wash, empty of water in the springtime, and admire our finds under her magnifying glass. We'd sunbathe in the pool, on yellow rafts, each wearing one of her bikinis. She bought me my first and second pair of cowboy boots, something she deemed important. She took me on day-long archaeology excursions with her professor friends. We admired her own artwork, collages usually, as well as new paintings and sculptures she'd picked up from artist friends in Sedona and Santa Fe. Every night for dinner, she would choose a different restaurant, noting that she had cooked enough in her lifetime, that she didn't want to do dishes, and that we ought to treat ourselves.

When I got older, if I was dating someone, she'd think he was just great. When we broke up, she'd say, like clockwork, "He wasn't right for you anyway."

From her, early on, I ingrained an overarching belief that good things are coming my way. They just are. Importantly, it's not just a thought; it is a *deeply held belief*. Because she knew that about herself, and because I diligently noticed how many good things happened to her and how she was surrounded with so much love and light, I chose to believe that about myself too.

Although my chronic illnesses threw me for a temporary negative loop in terms of my focus, I gradually began to remember, shore up, dust off, and polish to a high shine my overarching positive attitude that my life is blessed: that I am destined for love, greatness, and positivity. This attitude really had been with me since childhood, but during my well-being path, I intentionally began to amplify this umbrella-like, overarching viewpoint to bring more positive energy to myself. It was healing.

Although Birdie was alive at the time, I didn't tell her about my kidney cancer diagnosis. She was 98 years old, and I knew it would worry her too much. I did, however, channel her positivity the day of my surgery, a day I felt I needed it most. Even sitting in pre-op before my surgery at the UCSF Bakar Cancer Hospital, I kept myself amped up about my positive destiny by playing the *Rocky* theme song, "Gonna Fly Now,"[2] on my headset. By the time I was wheeled into the operating room, I had the entire surgical nurse team and my surgeon listening to it, all united in the belief that good things were bound to happen. After the four-hour surgery, my surgeon leaned over my rolling bed, smiled, and said, "This was the easiest surgery I have ever done. We saved ninety-five percent of your kidney, too."

I vowed to move through my life with a Birdie-inspired, open-hearted assumption that good things are likely, and that if they could happen to anyone, it might as well be me. I pray a soft pitch is coming right at me. I know that my innate strength in this spoke helped save my life and that Birdie's magical spirit still carries me along.

EMBODYING THE *MASTER A POSITIVE ATTITUDE* SPOKE

Mastering this spoke hinges on mastering the positive attitude and advanced belief that life is happening FOR your benefit and that the universe is conspiring to help you become everything that you were meant to be. Everything that is happening serves you in some way.

This is widely different than the belief that things are out of your control, that you are a helpless victim, and that you have no control of what is happening TO you. The unfortunate, "sh** happens" attitude doesn't serve anyone because the vibration is lower, un-empowered, and lifeless.

Having an overall positive attitude in place doesn't mean that you won't have tough times. Also, having a positive attitude doesn't mean that you recite platitudes to yourself about being happy when you authentically are not. It's very different from that. Having a positive attitude isn't so much DOING or saying positive things to yourself as it is a state of BEING—of *BEING* positive.

Having a positive attitude is a very high vibration that emanates a powerful frequency and a distinctly creative, expansive signal from your being. I believe it affects every cell of your body; it's a sacred gift.

How can this gift guide you to the best possible outcomes? I believe our experiences and circumstances can be manipulated by our underlying attitude because that powerfully emanating vibration touches everyone around us. I don't think it's a coincidence that Birdie inspired dozens of people to live life to the fullest, or that my cancer surgery exceeded the team's expectations. This is how life goes when you have a positive attitude. The mind is a powerful thing.

In researcher and psychologist Barbara L. Fredrickson's highly respected research paper "The Broaden-and-Build Theory of Positive Emotions," she convincingly shows us that rather than narrowing our mind-set like negative feelings do, positive emotions drive us to be our personal best in many ways. For instance, she argues that a positive attitude will "(i) broaden people's attention and thinking; (ii) undo lingering negative emotional arousal; (iii) fuel psychological resilience; (iv) build consequential personal resources; (v) trigger upward spirals toward greater well-being in the future; and (vi) seed human flourishing."[3] Wouldn't you want all of these upward-spiraling outcomes? Absolutely!

But what if things are spiraling downward in your life? What can a positive attitude do for you in a crisis? In the *New York Times* article "A Positive Outlook May Be Good for Your Health,"[4] writer Jane E. Brody connects positivity with greater health and longevity, and she inspires us with the concept that these skills can be learned and mastered. She cites, among many others, researcher Judith Moskowitz and her team at UCSF Medical Center, who studied newly diagnosed HIV patients and taught them ways to lift their outlooks. Moskowitz and her team discovered that "positive affect as a novel mechanism of change" helped the patients lower depression, reduce stress, and reduce mortality rates.[5] Even in crisis moments of high tension, such as a medical scare, deep positivity has a measurable impact.

There is an abundant, broadening power of a positive attitude. It expands you toward a greater and greater capacity for receiving everything you want in your life.

THE *MASTER A POSITIVE ATTITUDE* SPOKE AND WEALTH-BEING

This *Master a Positive Attitude* spoke remains one of the most valuable, behind-the-scenes power sources that I have.

As far as positive personal outcomes, I believe that the powerful inner dialogue of my positive attitude, which is like crucial software program running at all times, results in optimism as shown on the Wealth-Being Wheel. Because of my deep-seated belief that everything will be okay, carried by more than just the power of hope, I generated an empowering belief that everything I was going through would somehow *help* me become all that I was meant to be. I gathered a higher meaning and purpose from my path, and once I came out on the other side, it led me to bring my message of vibrant well-being to thousands of people.

Another positive personal outcome that cannot be underestimated is likeability. If you are filled with a positive vibration, it spills over. In the best possible way, it causes you to subconsciously know that *you* are taken care of, and therefore, it frees mental space for you authentically to care about the person in front of you. People want to be around positive people.

As far as positive professional outcomes on the Wealth-Being Wheel, my *Master a Positive Attitude* spoke most beautifully creates visionary thinking, because from the core of my being, I launch business ideas from a place of expansive possibility, of imminent potential. And because I have the core belief that things are happening on my behalf, to help me along, I assume the best. Have I had a dud business idea? Of course! Did I let it get me down? Thanks to my positive attitude, not for long.

Are you ready to polish up your positive attitude and soar? Let's do it!

CUSTOMIZING THE *MASTER A POSITIVE ATTITUDE* SPOKE FOR YOU

1. Let's have a quick, honest reality check to see where you're at. Are you a positive person overall? Are you a negatively oriented person? I am not speaking about situationally; I mean at your deep core. Be honest with yourself. If you cannot tell, ask someone close to you to provide an assessment.

2. If you have a negative bent and suffer from depression and anxiety, which I wholeheartedly believe are crushing and real, I recommend that you seek out professional help, therapy, and whatever else it takes to help improve your mental wellness. It is so important for your continued well-being.

3. Let's look at positive attitude influences around you. Begin by taking note of the five people whom you spend the most time with. Do you admire their positivity? Do they boost you, or do they unload a bunch of negative thinking in your lap? If you have a choice in the matter, boost time with the most positive, and diminish time with the more negative. Caveat: I know this can be easier said than done. For example, what if you have *a child* who is innately negative? In those types of situations, I believe you must move *toward* the negative person with love and compassionate understanding, provide professional help if needed, set the best possible example of positivity, and hope that someday it rubs off. In the meantime, you might need to over-fuel your positivity tank with the optimistic people to garner the strength for success with the negative ones.

4. Get in the habit of believing that your experiences are helping you become the best version of yourself. Don't brush this off. Really note your past challenges, for instance, and list two or three ways they helped you, built your resilience, increased your appreciation for the opposite, and so forth. Now note your current challenges. Train your mind to come from a sense of gratitude.

5. Note positive things, people, and experiences that you are easily grateful for, from the massive to the mundane. Many people keep a gratitude journal. If that speaks to you, do it.

6. Do more things that you think are fun; choose activities that generate that positive energy flow.

INCREDIBLE WELL-BEING CUSTOMIZATIONS FROM AN EXCEPTIONAL EXECUTIVE

Gopi Kallayil, Chief Evangelist, Brand Marketing, Google

Gopi recently created new personal cards. On one side, there's a widely smiling picture of himself. On the other side, it simply says "Happy Human."

He came up with this new, meaningful title after a visit to Dharamshala, a place in India on the edge of the Himalayas, where he met His Holiness the Dalai Lama. A huge fan of the Tibetan spiritual leader, Gopi notes that this in-person meeting was #36 on his bucket list of 100 top things he wants to experience in his life, and so when the opportunity presented itself, despite the 12,000-mile distance, he jumped on a plane.

Deeply affected by the Dalai Lama's obvious happiness and genuine laughter and delight, Gopi decided that above all, the "Happy Human" title is what he most aspires to. He says the new card, which he often shares with new acquaintances at one of the many conferences he keynotes at, has elicited many an enlivening conversation.

Another treasured title is "Author." Consequently, *The Happy Human: Being Real in an Artificially Intelligent World*[6] is the title of his second book, which was released by Hay House in 2018. The perfect Exceptional Executive for this well-being spoke, Gopi masterfully tackles this esoteric topic of happiness, which, for him, is deeply interrelated to having a positive outlook. Well-known as one of the most skilled storytellers in corporate America, Gopi hits his stride sharing unbelievably rich, both sad and hysterically funny, stories of his worldwide "flying leaps into the unknown" as a way of imparting how important it is to find meaning and purpose, how to stay grounded when your life crumbles, and how to find happiness within yourself.

His career title gives him somewhat of a rock star status at work, and his current role, with its immense impact, brings him joy. Gopi is Chief Evangelist, Brand Marketing, at Google, where he works with his teams and their customers to help business growth through digital marketing. Each week, his work varies greatly, from meeting with the CEO of Chrysler to presenting an on-site speech to the St. Jude Children's Research Hospital to participating in a Google Hangout meeting with Intel or any of the company's other big-name clients.

Before his current role, he was Chief Evangelist for Google+ in the Americas and Asia Pacific. He also did stints on the management teams at two venture-funded startups, and before that, he was a consultant at McKinsey & Co. Gopi earned his bachelor's degree in electronics engineering from the National Institute of Technology in India, and he has two masters degrees in business administration, one from the Indian Institute of Management, and the other from the Wharton School of Business at the University of Pennsylvania.

As an avid yoga practitioner, another title of positive significance to him is "Yoga Teacher," and every Monday, he teaches a free outdoor yoga class to his fellow Google colleagues. He founded this very popular program for his fellow "Yoglers," and it has grown to more than 200 classes per week. He proudly notes, "It's the largest corporate yoga program." Even with his worldwide travel schedule, he rarely misses this Monday yoga class, where he practices karma yoga, a Hindu-based belief focused on a consciously unselfish path of action. To that end, he says that instead of doing the downward dog and warrior poses along with the others, he walks around and looks for ways to be of service by helping correct postures and encourage students.

Funny and self-deprecating, he surveys the scene of his many well-earned titles and jokingly clarifies, "I am just a bricklayer here in Silicon Valley. It's true." No matter how he defines himself or how the world defines him, one thing remains intact at all times: his mastery of a positive attitude.

Gopi has come a long way from his humble beginnings in the rural village of Chittilancheri, India, and his family's rice fields, where his mother tongue is Malayalam. His long-running positive attitude of "why not?" and "what do I have to lose by trying?" created in him an insatiable curiosity about learning (he sits on the board of the Desmond Tutu Peace Foundation, which he finds mind opening), a desire to explore the world (in the fall of 2018, he was in nine cities and four countries, all in the course of 12 weeks), and a willingness to try anything that might expand him positively as a person (he spent eight hours on an autumn Saturday in downtown Los Angeles, performing kirtan music with a band he founded, noting that "we created an 'experience' "). He describes the music as yoga meets tech meets mindfulness.

His positive attitude leads him toward being a self-described "possiblearian," because he considers all possibilities doable or at least worth ruminating over, and as such, he reads incessantly, listens intently, and thrives in a work culture like Google, where innovations happen every day.

He finds another title, "Masterful Public Speaker," filled with possibilities. Having given more than 100 public speeches on everything from one's "inner-net" to social innovation to the business value of mindfulness, often to hundreds of people in the audiences, he's devoted to improving his persuasive speaking skills. Gopi competed in the 2018 Toastmasters World Championship of Public Speaking, which drew 36,000 contestants from more than 145 countries. He impressively placed second in the semi-finals, putting him in the top 20 overall for the competition. In true Gopi style, so absolutely true to his positive attitude, his speech was titled (with a nod to advice from his late father) "When a Door Opens, Walk Through It."

For his positive attitude to run optimally, he says that it helps if he takes his "MEDS," which stands for Meditation, Exercise, Diet, and Sleep. He targets eight hours of sleep nightly, which he admits is highly difficult, given his schedule, "which is like a treadmill set to 12 miles per hour." He ideally does one hour of physical activity daily; some days he does interval training (he's a triathlete), and other days he does his own yoga practice. Third, he targets meditating, "half an hour a day in two different segments." Finally, he follows a plant-based diet, which he describes as "primarily plant-based food, no carbohydrates, a good amount of protein, and good hydration." He adds that he does his best, and that he's "a practical vegetarian." Case in point, recently, having rushed to get the last seat in the back of a plane returning to California, he was starving. When the flight attendant made her way to his back row and told him the only food left was a turkey sandwich, he accepted it gladly. His positive attitude keeps him from suffering.

He says this four-part combination allows him to be "fully functional and in a peak state." This foundational base allows him to be happy and to allow life to unfold from there.

If things aren't working for him, like his lack of sleep, he's the first to admit "the relentlessness" of his schedule. Instead of giving in, he asks, "What is it that I can change?"

Why does Gopi care so much about personal happiness and about stoking the fire of his positive attitude? He feels that in the big picture, without self-acceptance, self-compassion (despite inevitable failures), and thus, genuine happiness, there is a dire emptiness that can come with achievement. Gopi has certainly amassed an incredible amount of achievement in his young life. He often sees empty, soul-less striving all around him, despite impressive titles and financial wealth and other trappings of success.

His advice to us is to first understand ourselves and discover what gives our life meaning. Oftentimes, in that dual knowing, we will find out what makes us happy. He masterfully curates a life to optimize both, aware of what props make him optimally perform, and he thinks we can do the same.

His attitude is that without happiness—without looking on the past, present, and possibilities of the future with positivity—what's the point? To know Gopi is to know someone with the most genuine, easy laugh: the ability to laugh at himself, to laugh at the craziness of what life brings us, and to laugh because that's who he inherently *is*—positive.

PART THREE

Universal SPIRIT Spokes

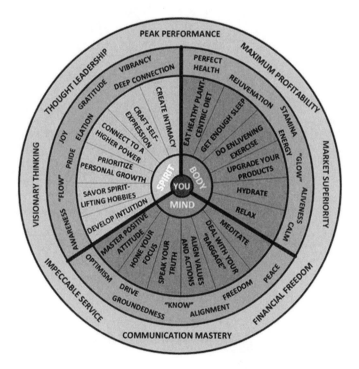

Develop Intuition: From Passing Illusions to Illustrative Insights

"Have the courage to follow your heart and intuition. They somehow already know what you truly want to become."[1]

—Steve Jobs

BLACK AND WHITE

When I was diagnosed with chronic kidney disease in addition to rheumatoid arthritis, I initially felt like I was looking at the world in black and white. On days when my overarching positive attitude moved so far into the background it was barely a whisper, everything seemed either good or bad: either something thrilled me (like a new client) or something made life extremely hard (like the standstill traffic). Looking back, I realize that it was a defense strategy, a judgmental sorting mechanism, and a reduced world view; I had shut out all nuances just to get by. Unknowingly, I disastrously shut down my intuition too.

By way of a miraculous suggestion, my sister, Mollie, who lives outside New York City, inadvertently helped me turn my life back from black and white to multicolor. To kick off her fortieth birthday year, she asked me to join her for a snowy January weekend at Kripalu, a stunning retreat center in the Berkshires of western Massachusetts, to take a four-day workshop on Reiki, a gentle Japanese healing art and beautiful spiritual practice founded more than 100 years ago by a Buddhist monk, Mikao Usui. *Rei* means "higher power," and *Ki* means "energy." Worried about my health, Mollie thought it might help heal me, plus she liked the whim of learning something totally new.

Excited to break my schedule and patterns, to learn a new type of healing practice (that might be just the thing), and to have some guaranteed fun with my sister, I immediately deemed this adventure as "good." Soon I was on a plane crossing the country.

As luck would have it, a divine teacher, Reiki Master Teacher Libby Barnett, MSW, set the exact heart- and spirit-opening tone we needed with her understanding and welcoming motherly manner. Under her guidance, that weekend changed both of our lives.

Reiki requires placing your hands on or right above yourself or the person whom you are working on, with the intention of delivering pure, healing, spiritual life force energy. As Reiki healers, Mollie and I became attuned in how to tap into that life force energy, and we learned how to get that concentrated healing energy coming out through our hands.

To my shock, what I truly learned that weekend was to wake up my intuition to the energy of people, the energy of all things, and the messages that the energy carries. In person after person who lay in front of us on the massage tables, we practiced reading their energy, tapping into subtleties, and listening to what our inner voice told us they needed. At first, being Miss Black-and-White, I came up blank and felt nothing. My sister, on the other hand, was a natural, embodying such ease and such receptivity it was breathtaking.

Mollie and my fellow students immediately sensed all sorts of information about people, such as a past arm injury or a deep sadness. How were they so tapped in? Feeling like a failure, I remember thinking, as was my pattern at the time, "This is bad." But after hours and hours of practice and sticking with it, suddenly my black-and-white veil was lifted, and my previous "this-or-that" broad categories made way for a glimpse of immensely bright, detailed, multicolored information.

I was amazed that suddenly I could sense so much. I could feel the person's energy, their buried emotions, if they were sick or not, their basic essence, and what they were all about. I could feel what they needed, and what words I could say that would boost them. The information coming to me had a very strong, true, absolutely-to-be-believed quality. Since we did Reiki on people first and then discussed it with them after, I received instant validation.

Astonished, I could barely contain myself without crying. To gather myself, I remember staring out the classroom's bay windows to the snowy fields. I felt a deep sadness for everything I had missed all these years—probably millions of clues about my failing health and beautiful kids and, by then, former husband—but also a profound thankfulness for my sister and this learning that cleared my vision and brought back my intuition.

Mollie and I loved that Reiki workshop so much that it became a spiritual calling. We sailed through Reiki Level I and II, and we were so devoted that on Mollie's actual fortieth birthday that year, we became Reiki Masters. I will never forget that perfect day at our induction ceremony. Our beloved teacher presided, and Mollie and I had tears of gratitude streaming down our faces. Ringing in our ears was the secret Japanese Reiki Master Word, a word so powerful it's believed to heal the healers.

EMBRACING THE *DEVELOP INTUITION* SPOKE

What really IS intuition? Known also as a sixth sense and an inner knowing, intuition can be a bit tricky to wrap your mind and heart around. As such, it seems that different people experience intuition in different parts of their body. Some have a gut feeling, while others seem to just "know it." Since that Reiki experience, I have been on a quest to deepen my ability to access this language and energy that had opened up for me.

I started reading, watching, practicing, and experiencing as much as I could. Luckily, there are a lot of extraordinarily wise sages in our midst.

In many of Sonia Choquette's books, particularly *The Psychic Pathway: A Workbook for Reawakening the Voice of Your Soul*, I learned that my intuition is my higher self. Sonia reinforced my experience that "intuition and psychic energy are subtle,"[2] and she stresses the importance of grounding, which is channeling your energy into the ground, reconnecting yourself to the earth and your solidity. She also recommends meditation, suggesting that "fifteen minutes a day of closing your eyes and clearing your mind is all that you will need to expand your awareness."[3] I loved that the previous MIND spoke, *Meditate,* was reappearing in my life.

In Laura Day's book *Practical Intuition: How to Harness the Power of Your Instinct and Make It Work for You*,[4] I learned that intuition is an instinct, a hunch that can be practiced, harnessed, and used every day. I did many of the exercises in her book.

In their stunning 2016 documentary *InnSaei: The Power of Intuition*, two Icelandic women filmmakers interviewed Bill George, a professor at Harvard University, who said, "We are complex beings, body, mind, and spirit, and when the pressure's on, we tend to just focus on the rational mind and we shut ourselves down. If we can't see inside ourselves, we can't use our greatest capabilities, and we never let our own intuition flow."[5] I can so relate to this.

The women also interviewed Iain McGilchrist, a British psychiatrist and author, who summed intuition up by warning that "to rule it out is to miss most of the wise things we could know."[6]

In his powerful 2018 documentary, *PGS—Intuition Is Your Personal Guidance System*,[7] Australian filmmaker Bill Bennett shares three years of interviews with leading scientists, authors, doctors, and spiritual teachers from all over the world.

One of his interviewees, Dr. Judith Orloff, who is a psychiatrist, a member of the psychiatry faculty at UCLA, and the *New York Times* bestselling author of *Second Sight*, explains that "intuition is a guidance system, it's the best friend you'll ever have, it's your inner voice, and you need to consult it with everything."[8]

From the perspective of going from inward to outward, another featured teacher, James Van Praagh, who is a celebrated spiritual teacher and the *New York Times* bestselling author of *Talking to Heaven*, shares an interesting point that "intuition guides us to our purpose and to fulfillment of our purpose."[9] He adds, "The more you understand your soul, the better."[10]

It's encouraging that so many incredible teachers and scholars agree on the importance of intuition. Without a doubt, intuition has become one of the most valuable, most accessed success tools I have.

THE *DEVELOP INTUITION* SPOKE AND WEALTH-BEING

As far as positive personal outcomes on the Wealth-Being Wheel, my awareness became heightened. As I mentioned, I began using my intuition to tap into everything in my personal life with the excitement of someone who is seeing things for the first time.

With my daughters, I used my intuition to be a better mom as I tapped into what they each might need, what words I should choose to comfort them or bring out their feelings about something, or even what fun things we should explore together on the weekends. I started teaching them everything I could about intuition, from how to read the energy of a potential new painting for our home collection to how to be an empathetic friend at school, and I realized immediately that because they are 10 steps ahead of me in terms of open-heartedness (as many kids are), instead they would be *my* teachers.

As far as positive professional outcomes on the Wealth-Being Wheel, my *Develop Intuition* spoke has been my guiding light as well as my differentiator. In my wealth management business, I serve senior corporate executives, and I use my intuition to guide them about when and how to sell their company stock, and where exactly to place the proceeds at what time. I am known among them for definitive guidance; many joke with me and say, "I need your magic touch." I use intuition to decide when it feels right to call a meeting in person, to see how else I might serve them.

The result is impeccable service, which leads to market superiority and then to financial freedom, as shown on the Wheel.

Intuition helped me define my overarching life's purpose, which is to bring vibrancy, healing, and inspiration to everyone I touch. Intuition nudged me (hard!) to start my entrepreneurial well-being and success-oriented venture in addition to my corporate career, and to take a major step in being of service to humanity with this book.

Are you ready to open up your intuition channels and experience this critical spoke? Get ready!

CUSTOMIZING THE *DEVELOP INTUITION* SPOKE FOR YOU

1. Practice being open to receive intuitive information. Sit somewhere comfortable and try this:
   a. GET NEUTRAL. Start with a clean slate. Try to be in as blank an emotional state as you can. You don't want to manipulate the incoming information with your intellectual preferences.
   b. PROTECT YOURSELF. Ask for only the highest, light-filled knowledge and wisdom to come through. I say exactly this: "Please give me the best, highest, most love- and light-filled advice."
   c. ASK. Directly invite your intuition to kick in by asking a question, such as, "What do I need to know?"
   d. LISTEN. Notice the first thing that you hear, that comes to mind, or that you feel. See if it feels true and benevolent, like good advice or good information.
   e. FOLLOW IT. The more you witness the successful outcomes of following your inner voice, the more you will rely on it.
2. Practice being in the present moment in general. Whatever you are doing, try to do only that. Be totally present. Intuitive hits

tend to come when we are fully in the now. You might find that for you, your intuition comes when you are in the shower or out in your garden. Be aware of your special places for insights.

3. Get outside more, and place yourself in nature. Nature, for many of us, is different than our day-to-day environment, and it can allow for an expansion of your senses—especially notice what you see, hear, feel, and touch. This sensitivity practice opens pathways to greater intuitive messages coming through.

4. Spend time alone. Be quiet. Observe what you notice in these moments. Attune yourself to notice the smallest things.

5. Try to look people in the eyes more, at home and at work. I feel this is a lost art, but there is tremendous information transmitted from people's eyes, and you can greatly expand your intuitive power from that one information source.

6. Start small, seeing if you can sense something like a parking space coming up or finding a coin on the ground between here and there.

7. Keep a journal of times you followed your intuition and the outcomes. It will be a list of near misses and triumphs to celebrate.

INCREDIBLE WELL-BEING CUSTOMIZATIONS FROM AN EXCEPTIONAL EXECUTIVE

Jen Groover, Serial Entrepreneur and International Speaker

One evening, when Jen Groover was at the grocery store with her newborn twins, she realized just how impractical the design of her handbag was. The girls were strapped in their infant carriers, and she had to place them next to her on the floor so she could dig through her handbag to find her credit card to pay. They both began screaming, and since she was holding the line up, Jen panicked and dumped her handbag full of

stuff in front of the cashier. She says, "I couldn't believe, as far as innovation has come in our society, that we, as women, accept a bucket for a
bag." She left the store thinking, "There has to be a better way."

Jen mulled over the idea, which kept coming into her awareness.
However, she hadn't ever created a product, nor did she have an artistic
or engineering background. Right out of college, she had worked as a
fitness instructor. She was tagged to be a national-level aerobics com-
petitor, and she ran a successful fitness coaching business.

She couldn't forget the grocery store incident, and says her intuition had her repeatedly asking herself, "What am I going to do about
this?"

Six months later, she was unloading her dishwasher when she was
struck with how the silverware basket neatly organized the knives, forks,
and spoons. In this unexpected, intuitive "aha" moment, she says, "I
thought to myself, 'This is how I want everything in my handbag to be—
standing up straight with a bird's eye view so I know where it is. . . . That
is what a handbag should look like on the inside.'" She pulled out the
silverware basket, placed it in her handbag, and her perfect solution, a
prototype for the Butler Bag, a revolutionary, compartmentalized handbag, was born.

Jen used her intuition to navigate the surprisingly change-averse
handbag industry, learning about everything from trademarks to pat-
ents, to design, to manufacturing, and to how to deal with the countless
naysayers who told her that women wouldn't resonate with her innovation. In business meetings, as she met with people who didn't share
her passion, she earnestly asked them, "What if? And why not?" which,
in a nutshell, symbolized her belief in herself and her inspired idea.
In 2010, this became the title of her bestselling book *What If? & Why
Not? How to Transform Your Fears into Action and Start the Business of
Your Dreams*,[11] which has resonated with thousands upon thousands of
admiring entrepreneurs who look up to Jen for inspiration, and who see
her as someone who strategically moves forward in just the right way.

Jen describes her intuition as "my highest self." She adds, "As I
get older, I trust it more and more. My mind taps into all sorts of crazy

things. I get downloads of consciousness that are beyond me. My intuition doesn't let me down."

Today, Jen recognizes that every time she has stumbled, it was because she didn't trust her intuition. For instance, as she embarked on her first licensing deal with the Butler Bags, she got a bad feeling about the man who owned the company, a sense that he didn't have the highest of ethics. However, his incredible level of conviction and his long list of celebrity clients convinced her to accept the outside validation. Fast forward, and the man, who had been secretly stealing from all his licensees, eventually went bankrupt, and Jen not only lost money, but also was left scrambling to rectify her valuable retailer relationships. She says the experience of "everything crumbling all at one time brought me to my knees to say 'I got it. I get the lesson here. Follow your intuition.' "

She says, "Thankfully, I intuitively forced myself into every retailer meeting to get to know those people from the start." She more than shored things up. In the first year, Jen's Butler Bags appeared in more than 100 stores with $1 million in sales. In the second year, she achieved $10 million in sales, and the Butler Bag went on to become one of the fastest-growing handbag lines in history.

Since then, Jen has launched many other lifestyle brands all fueled by her intuitive knowing. Tagged by *Success Magazine* as a "One-Woman Brand" and a "Creativity and Innovation Guru," Jen launched Jumpstart Connect, a full-service pop-up center for entrepreneurs seeking turnkey business services. Her LeaderGirlz brand fosters girls' leadership skills, confidence, and self-esteem through play. Empowered, a consumer products brand, encompasses her inspirational quotes and includes an Empowered Eyewear line; cleverly, wearers can use one pair of lenses but swap out different fashionable frames. Lastly, as a nod to her being a die-hard sports fan as well as a person who loves connecting to others in person, she's an advisor/partner in Thuzio, a private-event experience brand that honors professional sports icons in exclusive settings.

Jen says her special superpower is her ability to read people. She explains, "By being in alignment and being emotionally grounded, I am not easily affected by other people's stuff, and I can read their façade of who they want people to think they are and who they *truly* are. I very easily can see the deeper aspect of people." You can imagine how helpful this is in business dealings.

A frequent consultant to other high-level entrepreneurs, she says, "I can meet people and within seconds, tell them about their life, where they were, where they are, and where they should be going. It's the crux of what I do so effectively." If they are shocked by her accuracy, she explains to them that she is getting inner guidance that is incredibly strong and convicted. Sometimes what she says is so powerful it can create a new vision of belief beyond that person's current state, and, thus, change his or her life for the better.

Jen also uses this ability to read energy to assess a crowd. While many of her brands require significant behind-the-scenes work, to see her at her best is to witness her on a stage, giving a keynote address to hundreds of people. She frequently speaks about entrepreneurship and about taking your vision, bringing it to fruition, and pushing yourself to take everything further than you imagined. Also, she draws on her psychology degree and passion for philosophy to teach emotional intelligence, with the desire to awaken people to their highest, most thriving potential.

When speaking, she easily reads the overall audience vibe, whether it's fear-based and guarded or more receiving and encouraging. She also reads the body language of individual attendees, whether they are looking closed and sitting back or are engaged and leaning forward. A gifted speaker, she always has a couple of key points she wants to make, but she will read the room, adjust her speech and vocabulary accordingly, and go from there.

As she emphasizes, "Your intuition is one of your most powerful gifts. Your mind can create all kinds of crazy illusions, but your intuition will guide you with purity. To not respect its power and to not listen to it robs you and others of your destiny. Trust in yourself."

When Jen considers what being tapped in and aligned with that purity does for her, she takes a deep breath, as if to possibly encompass all that her intuition provides. Her conclusion? It has helped her achieve her greatest accomplishment, "consistent inner peace."

Savor Spirit-Lifting Hobbies: Getting in the Flow

"The treasures that are hidden inside you are hoping you will say yes."[1]

—Elizabeth Gilbert

SIX MISSING TEETH

It wasn't as if I planned it, but the day my first child arrived, my main spirit-lifting hobby stopped, suspended right there in time where I left it.

I have loved writing since I was a grade schooler in rural Northern Illinois. I crave the thrill of getting my thoughts and stories down on paper *in just the right way*.

I filled a thick journal each year with my musings about summer jobs in the cornfields and the unexpected freedom of life at an East Coast girls boarding school, and I went on to major in Creative Writing. From my professors, who were published authors and Pulitzer Prize winners, I learned to write in a more engaging way. I spent an unforgettable summer at Oxford studying the beautiful phrases of Wordsworth, and then, gripped with the power of the perfect story, I went on to get my Masters in Literature.

Writing came with me everywhere because it was *who I was*; I wrote about getting married, moving to California from Chicago, sharing an apartment where I could hear the Bay's fog horns at night, and traveling around the world with my husband. I wrote about the crystal-blue waters of Paros in the Greek islands, the day we met a sheep shearer in remote Turkey, and how we tipped the snake charmer in the souk in Marrakech.

I wrote almost every day, day in and day out, and it helped me to understand what I thought about the world; when my hand moved, my heart opened to my truth.

Later, though, when I was a first-time mom with a brand-new baby, my world upended. With all her extra care, the mere marvel of her adorable face, the awkward healing of my body, and the limitations of only 12 weeks of maternity leave (which I designated as the ideal time to study for the grueling Certified Financial Planner test to help my career), my spirit-lifting writing hobby went right out the window. I hate to admit it, but I was so incredibly distracted that I hardly noticed.

With such a new life paradigm, with so much more heaped on my plate, I had unintentionally let writing go, almost like a very favorite jacket accidentally cast aside and sent to Goodwill. I didn't notice it missing until I really needed it.

It wasn't until I took a deep-dive view of my life that I realized *I hadn't written a single creative writing word, not a single journal entry, in more than six years*. In my neat boxes of dated journals from every year since I was in grade school, there are six missing years, as obvious now as a row of missing front teeth.

It's not that I didn't chronicle that meaningful time; I have hundreds of photos of our baby, and then her sister two years later, and every adventure with our family of four. I even crafted scrapbooks detailing each and every memory, each about six inches thick. It was my love focused *outward*, not inward.

I certainly was a loving mother, a supportive wife, a good friend, and a rising star at work, but my identity as a writer was absent along with a sense of my deepest, truest self. The awareness felt like a self-inflicted gut punch—I had neglected the most passionate, alive, and attentive part of myself without a thought. Who was I? Who had I become? The undeniable, truest answer was…I was incredibly sick.

THE EMERGENCE OF THE UNIVERSAL
SAVOR SPIRIT-LIFTING HOBBIES SPOKE

This spoke wasn't so much created as reignited. My soul yearned for my favorite spirit-lifting hobby again, and once I had the insight that I needed to bring writing back into my life, I made it happen. I simply headed to the school supply section of the local store and bought a three-ring binder and some blank printer paper. This time, I sensed I needed more freedom and creative expression than a traditional, bound journal would offer.

My journal pages from that first year back were much more vibrant, alive, and passionate than before, bannered with sayings of things I wanted, like "Total Healing" and "Loving Kindness." I wrote page upon page of what I thought about my miserable illnesses, what they meant, strategies to get better, how I saw my life, and what I wanted from my future. It was obvious that simply writing again was bringing *me* back.

Matthew Zawadzki, a health psychologist at the University of California, Merced, presented, along with Joshua M. Smyth and Heather Costigan, a fascinating study for the *Annals of Behavioral Medicine* entitled "Real-Time Associations Between Engaging in Leisure and Daily Health and Well-Being." He showed that a mentally stimulating hobby provides positivity, happiness, genuine interest, reduced stress, and therefore "engagement in leisure has a wide range of beneficial health effects."[2]

Many others have also linked spirit-lifting hobbies to well-being. Xinyi (Lisa) Qian, PhD, Careen M. Yarnal, PhD, and David M. Almeida, PhD did a study for the US National Library of Medicine, National Institutes of Health,[3] which strongly showed that leisure time is an effective stress-coping resource that floods people with positivity.

Psychologist Mihaly Csikszentmihalyi, in his national bestseller *Flow: The Psychology of Optimal Experience*, describes these spirit-lifting hobbies as "flow activities," which "usually occur when a person's body or mind is stretched to its limits in a voluntary effort to accomplish something difficult and worthwhile."[4] Have you ever been so immersed in an activity that time seemed to stop, your concentration kicked in, your consciousness vanished, and it felt blissful? You experienced flow. I have loved this book for years.

His work shows that "in the long run optimal experiences add up to a sense of mastery—or perhaps better, a sense of *participation* in determining the content of life—that comes as close to what is usually meant by happiness as anything else we can conceivably imagine."[5]

So what's getting in our way? Why is this spoke the one that almost every high achiever has on the back burner? One problem is that many of us in the workforce think that there isn't time in such a busy day for something as frivolous as a hobby; after all, many of us loved those hobbies as kids, but now recess is nonexistent, and childhood is over.

Another problem is that many of us in the workforce know we need a break from our stressful day, but we select the default, the thing with the least effort: wasting time on social media, web surfing, or binge-watching TV series shows. It's basically passive; we watch the content move by, sucked into its addictive, colorful nature, and at the end, we know deep down we are no better for it.

In contrast, a spirit-lifting hobby is active, engaging, and energizing, and we rise a notch every time we do it. It's different than relaxing. It's using downtime for a productive, uplifting purpose. That sounds good to me. I'm in!

THE *SAVOR SPIRIT-LIFTING HOBBIES* SPOKE AND WEALTH-BEING

What did vastly improving my *Savor Spirit-Lifting Hobbies* spoke do for me?

On the positive personal outcomes ring of the Wealth-Being Wheel, I immediately felt joy again, the pure pleasure of rediscovering the thing that I love to do. For many of us, reigniting that hobby will feel like coming home, and it's really coming home to our truest nature. It welcomes us with open arms.

Because of my writing training, my lifelong desire to be a writer, I also feel "flow," because I am building on the mastery that Csikszentmihalyi astutely references. It's so true. For me, writing is a pleasure with a purpose, and I am better for it. When I sit on my king-size bed every evening, paper on a clipboard on my lap, I get better and better at writing with truth about my life.

A spirit-lifting hobby can also make you more compelling and interesting as a person. When I first started my career 20-plus years ago, it was a badge of honor to say I spent the weekend indoors working, but now, let's be honest, that causes people to cringe. Now the consensus is that people who do this tend to be one-dimensional, boring, and extraordinarily difficult to connect with.

Spirit-lifting hobbies can be solitary, like my writing, but when they involve others, they can actually create like-minded community and positive connections. Because my daughters and friends share some of my common, passionate interests, I have an exponential amount of flow and joy with them whenever we engage in some of my other spirit-lifting hobbies: seeing Broadway shows in New York City, trying new restaurants and exploring the California coast (my favorite stretch in the world).

As far as positive professional outcomes on the Wealth-Being Wheel, my *Savor Spirit-Lifting Hobbies* spoke has brought me a tremendous and unexpected amount of thought leadership. I am much more tapped in to knowing who I am and what I offer—just the act of writing every day about my experiences and reactions to them allows quicker access to my meaningful opinions. This is tremendously helpful for me in business, especially when I have daily client interactions that require a high level of emotional intelligence delivered in a professional manner.

This spoke has also brought me to a new level of visionary thinking. Because writing in itself is a creative endeavor, I am dipping into that creative well regularly, and it is a highly expansive habit. Visionary thinking requires thinking outside the box, and in my career world of finance, that creativity can get stifled. I am so much more adept now at helping clients create their vision for their future; we actively imagine it together and I can much more easily craft written plans and beautifully diversified portfolios for their financial freedom. I can't help but describe the whole thing as a work of art.

Are you ready to experience this game-changing spoke? Let's go.

CUSTOMIZING THE *SAVOR SPIRIT-LIFTING HOBBIES* SPOKE FOR YOU

1. Do you engage in a spirit-lifting hobby now? Does it work well for you? Does it require the right amount of attention, concentration, and challenge that allows you to experience flow? Does it give you joy? If yes, let's call that a winning customization for you. Keep doing that!

2. Think back on your life. Is there something you used to deeply enjoy but you've stopped doing? Could there be a way for you to bring it back? Note: Even if it is physically impossible for you now (e.g., motorcross racing), write it down and examine it. Don't immediately discount it. In this example, instead of racing yourself, could you possibly enjoy being an active spectator?

3. Is there something that you have always wanted to try? Start researching how you might be able to learn about it and get it started in your life. Are there local classes? An online class?

4. Are you up for taking a chance, shaking things up, and doing something unexpected? It could lead to a lifelong spirit-lifting hobby! Almost every community has adult classes on everything from tap dancing to bird watching, and it might be fun to pick one of interest to you.

INCREDIBLE WELL-BEING CUSTOMIZATIONS FROM AN EXCEPTIONAL EXECUTIVE

Riley Etheridge Jr., Former Managing Director, Client Segments & Solutions, Merrill Lynch Wealth Management; Rock Ridge Music Recording Artist; Senior Consultant

It's late afternoon, he's finished work for the day, and singer-songwriter Riley Etheridge Jr. is standing in front of a window in his condo in the Chelsea district of New York City. The new vistas from 24th Street connect him to the artsy vibe of the nearby brick-façade galleries, coffee shops (he knows them all), and general neighborhood. He's about to start his daily practice, and of the eight or so guitars he keeps in the condo, he says he "always makes sure to keep at least one guitar out so I don't have any excuse for not picking it up, even if it's only going to be for fifteen minutes." He straps on his current favorite, one he bought used and well broken-in from the small-production, boutique guitar maker Santa Cruz Guitars.

When he's at his other home, which is located in Los Angeles, he follows the same late-afternoon practice, but instead of enjoying the Chelsea view, he looks out at his beautiful, Southern California garden. In fact, he even has one of his *other* well-worn Santa Cruz Guitars there to play. He laughs and admits he's a creature of habit.

Riley says that practicing and playing his guitar "is a foundation for my well-being" and that "for me, it's almost like meditating because it consumes me, it absorbs me, and it creates a dynamic where I am in the flow and I am not thinking about what I need to do next or what happened before. I get enveloped in the process of either trying to play something I don't know or improve something I do, and I find that very centering. It's a level of focus and engagement that I don't find in many other areas of my life."

One of Riley's favorite reads is Csikszentmihalyi's *Flow*, particularly the description of "challenges to expand ourselves."[6] Riley notes that his own flow doesn't occur because he's a professional musician or so skilled at the guitar: "I think it's the opposite. I want to learn and improve; it's that pushing against the limits of what I am capable of. I find that when I am playing something that I wrote a long time ago or perform a lot, that doesn't have the same effect that intentional, conscious practice does."

His original music genre is Americana, mixed with a little country, rock, blues, soul, folk, and Cajun styles, a nod to his birthplace of Columbia, South Carolina, and the 20 years he lived in Baton Rouge. Critics say he sounds like a combination of Lyle Lovett and John Hiatt, and he does.

When Riley is preparing for an upcoming show with his four-person band, where he plays guitar and is also the lead singer, he either spends the time learning a new song for the show or trying to play more expressively something he already knows. He admits, "Learning to play well and perform is an art in itself, and there's no shortcut for that other than the repetition of playing a lot."

If you have seen him play for a sold-out crowd at the Rockwood Music Hall in New York City, you may find it hard to believe that Riley Etheridge Jr. held one of the top senior executive positions at Merrill Lynch Wealth Management, where he had a legendary 30-year career and was a widely beloved leader. What is most astonishing and unique about Riley is that his meteoric career rise to the top leadership positions at Merrill Lynch *coincided* with the impressive rise in his music career.

In fact, Riley has always brought his spirit-lifting musical skills along with him. He honed his drumming skills while majoring in history at Louisiana State University, and for his first 10 years in the workforce, he worked as one of Merrill Lynch's top financial advisors *and* played two or three music gigs per week with his Baton Rouge–based band.

A year after taking on leadership of Merrill Lynch's highly specialized Private Banking and Investment Group in New York City, he came out with his first independently produced album, *Things I Used to Know* (2009).[7] The album got significant attention, and he signed a recording deal with Rock Ridge Music. He then released *Powder Keg* (2011),[8] a studio EP titled *Better Days* (2012),[9] and *The Arrogance of Youth* (2012).[10]

When he was promoted to Merrill Lynch's Managing Director and Head of Client Segments and Advisor Development, a C-suite position at the firm, he shouldered three huge responsibilities: private banking, the goals-based wealth management strategy team, and the training of more than 14,500 financial advisors. During those years, he simultaneously released the more freewheeling *The Straight and Narrow Way* (2014)[11] and his fifth full-length album, the more mellow *Secrets, Hope & Waiting* (2016).[12]

The interesting thing about Riley is that during this, the height of his career at Merrill Lynch, or now as he continues to consult, he just as easily could be on tour with his band, performing at the House of Blues in New Orleans, as he could be giving the keynote address at the Barron's 100 Conference. Either way feeds his soul, he says, because "there is a sense of connection with the audience." Between both careers over the past 30 years, he has presented his skills in front of thousands upon thousands of people.

How does he do both, much less do them as well as he does? He says there is a connection between the productivity he's bringing to his simultaneous executive career and to his professional music career: "In the things I have chosen to commit time to, I have found that working hard, improving and producing work in one domain definitely feeds the other. For me, *momentum creates momentum*. I find that the more I am in the world interacting, learning, meeting new people, and being inspired by things in either domain, the more productive I actually become in anything I am doing."

Viewed in this way, it's clear that he doesn't just *play* music, he *leverages* music. See how that works for him?

Also, like many Exceptional Executives, Riley doesn't waste much time away from work. He writes his lyrics on airplanes, where, he says, "the quiet isolation helps me focus. I often quickly record new melody or chord progression ideas on my iPhone voice memo app, and I can use travel time to edit."

Also, his spirit-lifting passion has a twofold benefit: it has that solo flow element, when he practices daily, and a community connection flow element. He connects with his band, which is made up of phenomenal musicians and longtime, dear friends. He explains, "While I do some solo shows, they are not nearly as satisfying for me as playing with the people who are in my band. The interplay with them, the communication with the harmonies, improvisation—there's just a real sense of connection that I am super-grateful for and that just doesn't happen any other way for me."

Of course, Riley connects with his audience as well, saying, "I am always happy to have a chance to just play for the audience and hopefully connect with them in a way that's meaningful."

For those of you who think your career is bound to suffer if you decide to fill your free time with a spirit-lifting hobby, Riley disagrees. He encourages us all and, speaking for himself, says, "I don't think *anything* has suffered. At least nothing in my priority set. I find the activities to be mutually supportive. I loved it when the networks I built in one domain crossed over and I saw new relationships form. It was a conscious choice as I was building out the things I wanted to spend time on."

Riley is a supreme example of how the power of a spirit-lifting, free-time passion can empower our well-being and our at-work career to unimaginable heights. In his case, it's primarily sourced from the immense power of this one spoke, leveraged to perfection.

Riley urges us all to do the thing our soul craves, the activity that sparks us with life. To take a quote from the lyrics of one of his most popular songs from *The Straight and Narrow Way*, this hobby could be your "second chance" and your "saving grace."[13]

Prioritize Personal Growth: Enlightening Expansion

"Outside the cage, the sun is roaring with fission, arching through the blue sky. Wild winds flap the flags and fill the air with the sound of songs caught up in ecstasy and longing. There is life in its fleshy and toothsome grandeur...all of it on the one hand waiting for us to act, and on the other rushing down the hourglass."[1]

—Gregg Levoy

MARTYR SYNDROME

It took a lot of motivating self-talk and a lot of guts to get to the brave moment when I asked my husband a question I had been wanting to ask for months: "Do you think it would be okay if I checked into the Claremont for a night?"

The Claremont is a beautiful, white, wedding-cake-like hotel nestled in the Berkeley, California, hills, about 15 minutes from our home. To me, the hotel epitomizes spotless beauty, slow self-care, gentle luxury, and peace. At the time, I imagined a blissful night to myself, prioritizing my personal growth by reading a favorite book, watching a movie I had missed, and ordering lemon butter salmon from room service. I hadn't done any of those things in *years*.

My husband immediately sensed what I meant, and he was incredulous. "You mean, check in by *yourself*? *Without us*?" He gestured to our girls. Madeline was toddling over to play with her colorful dollhouse, and Amelia was crawling across the carpet toward a stuffed dragon. Just the genuine sadness in his voice made me recoil. I wanted to leave them on their own? I didn't want to *be* with them?

I wished I hadn't asked. The ridiculousness of it slapped me across the face. My internal self-talk was harsh and swift. Who did I think I was, asking for something that selfish, not to mention expensive? I couldn't carry through. I immediately bailed. "I'm just kidding. I just meant…"

He sighed, clearly relieved. "Whew!"

During this time, when I was struggling to get my chronic pain under control, when I was struggling to care for my daughters while working full time, when I connected with my husband in the sliver of time after the girls fell asleep and we went to bed, I hardly ever had any time alone. In fact, my only time alone was usually in the shower and in my car on my commute to work, but during the latter, I maximized the time by taking work calls.

Consequently, I was constantly yearning to have some time every day for myself. In that solace, I imagined, I could not only recharge but also reboot that part of myself that loved to learn, expand, and grow. It had gone missing as I focused solely on the people who depended on me. I had witnessed my own mother put everyone else's needs before hers while I was a child, and I had vowed back then to never do that, but here I was, not strong enough to stand up for myself, and having to admit that I, too, had become a professional martyr.

I wish I could say that I had the personal strength back then to carve out some consistent alone time for personal growth along the way. I wish that I had been able to show my family that a Megan recharged and growing was much better than a Megan depleted and declining, but I struggled to find the strength to upset the deeply grooved pattern that had been established.

THE INSTANT SPOTLIGHT OF THE UNIVERSAL *PRIORITIZE PERSONAL GROWTH* SPOKE

This spoke came into being about six years later, after my husband and I moved to different homes. At that point, the girls began spending time with each of us separately—half the time with him, and half the time with me—so I suddenly had a few days a week to myself. At first, being alone was excruciating. The house was silent, and I missed the girls' smiles and hugs. However, I quickly embraced reality and realized that I could reclaim and even honor this sudden arrival of free time in a myriad of ways. Once I got grounded around the idea, it felt like stepping into a personal spotlight. There was suddenly time for me.

In the words of Viktor E. Frankl, a noted neurologist, a Holocaust survivor, and the author of one of my favorite books, *Man's Search for Meaning*, "When we are no longer able to change a situation, we are challenged to change ourselves."[2] I changed myself by jump-starting my personal growth.

Personal growth is an ongoing process of challenging and moving yourself forward as you embrace new wisdom, fresh knowledge, and exciting experiences that interest you, that speak to your passions, and that ultimately make you a more interesting, more multidimensional, and more fulfilled person. Personal growth involves embracing new material and trying new things.

"Every success story is a tale of constant adaptation, revision and change,"[3] says British billionaire, disruptive entrepreneur, and impact philanthropist Sir Richard Branson. Our success is moved forward by our willingness to grow personally.

Personal growth enhances well-being because it nudges you closer to the best possible version of yourself. As adults, it's helpful to remember that personal growth is often self-induced learning—often, we are no longer in a school structure with a laid-out curriculum, so we need to be self-motivated to seek out ways to continue to expand and grow.

Adelaide Anne Procter, a mid-1800s British poet and philanthropist, said, "We always may be what we might have been."[4] I agree wholeheartedly. I began my journey to prioritize personal growth right from where I was at that point. I focused on two specific categories: *at home* and *away*.

At home, I started with books. I first sifted through a wish list of titles I had been keeping for the previous few years. Excited about this possibility, I even created a document with tiny colored pictures of the covers of every book I wanted to devour that year, and as I finished each one, I wrote the date next to it. I was so hungry to reclaim topics that interested me, to savor and satisfy my curiosity about the world, and to expand myself.

Away, I began to seek out retreats and workshops on a wide range of subjects all meant to aid my personal growth. The combination of the travel to an amazing new place, with brand new people to meet, and the fascinating topic at hand thrilled me so much that I started making plans months in advance.

I learned about psychic power and Native American drumming at Miraval Resort at the base of the Catalina mountains of Tucson, Arizona. I learned about sacred kirtan chanting from Grammy Nominee Snatam Kaur at the Kripalu Center for Yoga and Health in the Berkshire mountains of Massachusetts. I learned a freestyle form of dancing called "Soul Motion" at Esalen Institute, and we danced in a building overlooking the breathtaking ocean views of Big Sur, California. I have been to all of these retreat locales multiple times for dozens of growth-inducing, soul-expanding workshops.

Both at home and away, nurtured with books and new learning experiences, I replanted myself and began to re-grow in the most colorful, energetic, gratifying ways.

THE *PRIORITIZE PERSONAL GROWTH* SPOKE AND WEALTH-BEING

Rebooting my *Prioritize Personal Growth* spoke moved me toward the positive personal outcome on the Wealth-Being Wheel of pride. I hadn't felt pride about my own personal growth in a long time. When you intentionally carve out time for you, embracing topics that you're dying to dive into, you send a signal to your being that you are worth it, and that you matter. When you learn a new talent, explore an unfamiliar topic, or experience a new culture, you reinforce the feeling of being a capable, interesting person who has achieved something meaningful and personal. It builds confidence.

Prioritizing personal growth gives you a pride-filled spring in your step in the best possible way. People are attracted to that joy and livelihood. I noticed that my daughters and friends were much more interested in what unexpected new topic I was exploring as opposed to how my work was going.

As far as positive professional outcomes on the Wealth-Being Wheel, my *Prioritize Personal Growth* spoke consistently helped me to sharpen my mind, skills, talents, and knowledge behind the scenes. My financial services career, in general, requires linear thinking, flawless A-to-Z planning, and analytical skills. Because I intentionally seek out mostly creative endeavors in my personal-growth projects, and because they are so different, I learned to be more fluid and more expansive at work, and I believe that has helped me imagine new possibilities for clients, which translates to thought leadership.

Having a new project or interest has certainly made me more relatable and more fun to connect with—which cannot be underestimated in business, and which I would catalog under communication mastery. Clients seem interested in hearing that I have a vibrant life.

Entrepreneur, philosopher, and author Jim Rohn said, most profoundly, "Income seldom exceeds personal development."[5] By prioritizing this spoke and understanding this undeniable connection, you create a win-win for your well-being and an open door for your income potential, which refers to financial freedom. What's not to love about that?

Are you ready to plan for this up-leveling, spirit-enhancing spoke?

CUSTOMIZING THE *PRIORITIZE PERSONAL GROWTH* SPOKE FOR YOU

1. Let's first assess the state of your personal growth. Is it a priority, something that gets a so-so amount of attention, or is it non-existent? Be honest with yourself.

2. Let's take a quick look at WHY you answered as you did in the first question. For instance, if you answered "so-so" or "non-existent," do you have other responsibilities crowding out this time? Are you reluctant to take time for yourself? Why?

3. I believe it helps to start with some diehard inspiration. Think about what topic, place, or experience you would like to pursue if given the chance to enhance your personal growth. Any come to mind? What has caught your attention?

4. Now it's time to fit it in. If this is an area that needs improvement for you, why not start small? Could you devote, say, 10 minutes a day to this? Or maybe a half an hour on a day off?

5. I believe this spoke organically grows in the form of a welcome habit, a treat that you look forward to. You could start scheduling a little bit a day, so that it will become so welcomed and fun that you will intuitively find ways to make it happen. It feels good to grow and expand. Experiment.

6. Interested in reading up on this topic? One of my favorite writers of all time, Gregg Levoy, has two masterpieces, and you cannot go wrong with either. The first book is *Callings: Finding and Following an Authentic Life*[6] and the second is *Vital Signs: The Nature and Nurture of Passion.*[7]

INCREDIBLE WELL-BEING CUSTOMIZATIONS FROM AN EXCEPTIONAL EXECUTIVE

Chip Conley, Founder, Modern Elder Academy; Strategic Advisor for Hospitality & Leadership, Airbnb; and Founder and Former CEO, Joie de Vivre Hospitality

Chip Conley found himself onstage recently at LinkedIn's headquarters with Christina Hall, LinkedIn's Chief People Officer, discussing why today's workplaces need more "modern elders." With his perennially tan face (from his newest learning curve—surfing in Baja, Mexico), his jeans, his favorite funky blue-and-tan shoes, and his relaxed manner, he hardly seems elder, but because his personal-growth trajectory and multiple successes have earned him so much wisdom over the years, he says he's proudly reclaiming the word to celebrate that "wisdom is a path to growing whole, not old."

In addition to "modern elder," Chip is often referred to as a "rebel entrepreneur," a "hospitality industry disruptor," and an "authority on the intersection of psychology and business." The consistent theme running through it all? His commitment to personal growth and to expansion. Chip says, "For me, well-being is how you create the conditions in the long run—not the short run—to flourish."

Chip is a lifelong passionate learner. He says, "I am extremely curious. Curiosity engages me in a present way."

He attended Stanford as an undergraduate and then Stanford Business School, and soon after, he combined his love for commercial real estate with his knack for creating exceptional experiences for people as the Founder and CEO of Joie de Vivre Hotels. At age 26, he started with an inner-city motel, The Phoenix, in San Francisco's Tenderloin district, and for the next 24 years, he grew the brand to employ more than 3,500 people in what became the second largest boutique hotel chain in the United States. A subject of constant interest, Chip says he consciously nurtured the business environment so that he and his employees would be inspired to "do the best work of our lives at the company."

He proudly explains, "The name of the company, which means 'Joy of Life,' and the mission statement were the same. Very few companies can say that."

During his reign at Joie de Vivre, Chip received The Pioneer Award, the hospitality industry's highest honor, and was named "The Most Innovative CEO" by the *San Francisco Bay Area Business Times*. In 2010, seeking new opportunities for personal growth, he sold the company, which he still calls his "baby."

Chip filled his sudden free time with a way to expand personally. Since he embraces travel, describes himself as "culturally curious," and simultaneously believes that "the more digital we get, the more ritual we need," in 2013 he visited 20 countries to experience their unique festivals. His expansion covered five weeks and five festivals in Asia, including the Kumbh Mela, a Hindu religious festival with upwards of 150 million pilgrims, which is considered to be the world's largest human gathering. He says, "Being at that place in my life at the time where I had space to do it, I am so glad that I did. It was a passion project." He adds that prioritizing personal growth to pursue a passion project "can be life changing."

Those experiences inspired him to create another company, Fest300, "to cultivate curiosity and to bring [my] love of festivals to the world." Fest300 merged with Everfest in 2016, and it now offers a full travel-planning experience platform for a wide choice of US and world-wide festivals, ranging from music, film, arts, holiday, book, food, and many others. Chip remains the Chief Strategy Officer. Also, as a nod to his love of festivals, he sits on the board of directors of the Burning Man Project, the yearly Nevada desert festival attended by more than 70,000 people annually. He appreciates the leadership aspect of being involved, but also, he says, he enjoys, "simply experiencing the beauty of aesthetics to the point of awe, like being at Burning Man at nighttime and seeing the lights and appreciating that there's so much there."

It wasn't long after his year abroad when an enticing learning opportunity lured him out of his self-imposed retirement. At first, he came to Airbnb to mentor the cofounder and CEO, Brian Chesky, but his initial

15-hour-a-week commitment soon became more than full time as he was named Airbnb's Head of Global Hospitality & Strategy. Chip readily admits he actually felt more like an intern among the whip-smart, passionate employees, many of whom were half his age. In situations like this, Chip's passion for personal development dramatically sets him apart, and it consistently sets him up for success. He moves *toward* learning experiences, he values his innate curiosity over discomfort, and he consistently embraces change. He finds a way to become a valuable asset, always.

For the next four years at Airbnb, Chip's deep-seated wisdom about the hospitality industry and scaling served the company well, and he oversaw a number of business units, including Hospitality, Leadership and Development, and Business Travel. During this period, he says, CEO Chesky described him as "the defacto Secretary of State of the travel industry for Airbnb." He still remains a Strategic Advisor for Strategy and Leadership.

Chip explores and masters topics of interest by writing about them, and he is a *New York Times* bestselling author of five acclaimed books. Inspired by the work of well-known psychologists Abraham Maslow and Viktor Frankl, he wrote his books *PEAK*[8] and *Emotional Equations*[9] to share his vision of transformation and meaning in life and business. His book *Wisdom@Work: The Making of a Modern Elder*[10] is both a memoir and a playbook about successfully recreating yourself in midlife. He is the perfect conduit to deliver this message, especially at this moment in time when our workforces have the opportunity to employ four generations. Chip feels that at our best, we are all learning from each other.

In early 2018, combining his mastery of the hospitality industry with his passion around helping others grow personally, he founded Modern Elder Academy (MEA), the world's first midlife wisdom school. The school is located in Baja California Sur, Mexico, where he embraces participants with his warm nature (he's always one to hug people) and infuses them with a welcome feeling of belonging.

There, on a stunning expanse of beachfront property, where Chip lives on a part-time basis, the guests, who fall mostly between the ages of forty-five and sixty-five, immerse themselves in a week-long workshop designed to help them evolve, learn, collaborate, and counsel along a new, reframed, and self-defined midlife path.

Chip also believes public speaking is a way to master topics and, even more fun for him, to connect to audiences. As one of the most sought-after keynote speakers in the United States, he received a standing ovation for his speech at TED national, has done several TEDx presentations, has given a keynote presentation at a massive Zappo's all-hands meeting, and is a beloved speaker at the annual Wisdom 2.0 gathering of 3,000 people. He says the thrill of challenging himself with speaking "is the combination of science and art. The science is that structure [of the speech], and the art is the presence, the ability to connect with an audience, from a place of not just telling the right stories but also of bringing in the spirit."

Chip take a theoretical step back and says, "I want to live a life filled with joy and share that with other people—to help create that in other people's lives. Joy is something that isn't circumstantial, but rather something that springs from within. It's an unusual way of framing a CEO's life." He explains further, "There are a lot of people who see it as success driving joy, but as I have said many times, it's the opposite. Joy comes from care and cultivation."

Chip sets an incredible example for those interested in prioritizing personal growth. He ruminates on his expansive interests, but also on the unexpected growth that comes from spending time without a goal attached, like taking a bike ride down a country road where he doesn't know where he's going. He's genuinely delighted as he admits, "I do some crazy stuff."

Connect to a Higher Power:
Plugging In for Increased Wattage

"We hope that God's world will become a better
place, more hospitable to goodness, more hospitable
to compassion, more hospitable to generosity, more
hospitable to living together."[1]

—His Holiness the Dalai Lama and
Archbishop Desmond Tutu

ON MY OWN

In the midst of my health crises, my inflammation markers had risen
to more than six times normal, I was getting blood tests weekly, and
I was being seen regularly by top-notch traditional and outstanding alternative medicine doctors at the UCSF Medical Center. Toward
the end of an appointment, after reviewing my supplements and my
diet, my alternative medicine doctor asked, "Do you have a spiritual
practice?"

Completely caught off guard, I answered with the first thing
that came to mind, about how I used to be Catholic. He answered,

compassionately, that perhaps an inactive religious affiliation would not qualify as a spiritual practice.

Back in my car on the way home, I turned off my radio, drove in the silence, and pondered that question. It stuck with me because it caused in me a shock of introspection, where I simultaneously felt not only a deep sense of guilt for abandoning my religion those past seven years but also a curiosity that perhaps this was the essential missing piece that might move me toward well-being.

I grew up in a strict, Catholic family in the rural Midwest, where church every Sunday was an undebatable requirement, and my deepest memories are of the itchy wool dress clothes, the choking thick incense, the (to me, unfair) rule that girls were not allowed on the altar during mass, and the awkwardness of confession, where I had to come up with one or two sins to tell the priest, who said that I was forgiven but that I better go back to the pew and say some Hail Marys as penance. Confused, I always thought it would be better if I apologized directly to the person I hurt; how would they even know I was sorry?

Despite these challenges, through grade school, high school, and college, from my Catholic upbringing I carried in my heart a beautiful, deep-seated belief in God as an overarching divine presence, and in Jesus as a gifted healer and spirit who exemplified acceptance and unconditional love. What a gift to grow up learning I was always watched over. I prayed to them anytime I needed help.

In my late twenties, when I fell in love and married an atheist, the lack of a shared religious connection put my prayer life solely into my corner, and it became a private personal practice until it diminished in importance year by year. Perhaps it was due to the focus of my career, or the interesting myriad of beliefs we encountered in our world travels, or the busy excitement of having our two daughters, or the new, complete absence of time alone, but somehow, other thoughts took the place of prayer. For almost seven years, I didn't seek divine help or blessings. I didn't pray. As I drove home from that doctor's appointment that day, I had to admit that I had not thought about God in years.

I was completely on my own. And sick.

THE REVAMP OF THE UNIVERSAL *CONNECT TO A HIGHER POWER* SPOKE

The doctor's question shocked me into remembering my faith, and I wondered if a belief in a higher power could be the missing piece here that could help solve my critical health problems. Maybe I needed God's intervention. "I am a woman of action," I thought, "and I can start with some earnest prayers."

However, my soul seemed to be calling me to do more than desperately revive prayers. If the Catholic church didn't resonate, what else might? Was there a community or a belief system that might support what I truly believed rather than what I was raised to believe?

Discovering our unique expression of a connection to a higher power is just that—unique. What resonates with each of us may be totally and completely different, may be affected by our upbringing, and may be influenced by who we are now. Regardless, its power is in a quality of wonder, an experience of unconditional love. Further, it's about us expanding beyond ourselves.

I love Rabbi Rami Shapiro's sentiment of openness, "I am at heart a *Jnana* yogi: my path is wisdom, and I find wisdom in silence but also in text. Ideas matter to me. They are seeds that can blossom into compassion and awareness, and I plant them in my mind through study and recitation."[2] I became open to wisdom.

While I continued to study meditation at the Spirit Rock Meditation Center in Woodacre, California, I became drawn to their wide range of riveting, well-taught Buddhism classes. There I learned all about Theravada Buddhism, a major tradition of Buddhism practiced mainly in Burma, Thailand, Cambodia, and Laos. A modern expression of this is the Vipassana movement, or Insight Meditation movement.

Buddhism's teachings on loving kindness, self-compassion, and mindfulness deeply resonated with me. I often brought all of my frustration about my lack of well-being, as well as my spiritual emptiness, to those classes. Besides learning the details of the Eightfold Path (and I took pages of notes), I frequently experienced newfound waves of soothing self-acceptance as I recited the metta traditional phrases: "May I be filled with lovingkindness. May I be safe from inner and outer dangers. May I be well in body and mind. May I be at ease and happy."[3]

I immediately connected to the open and friendly Buddhist sangha, and for the first time in my life, I experienced a spiritual community where I felt at home. I even spent several New Year's Eves celebrating with this group, all of us dancing the night away, and all of us witnessing the 108 breathtaking gongs at midnight, ringing in the new year.

I love the following old story, told of the Buddha. Soon after the Buddha's enlightenment, a man passing him on the road asked, "Are you a man, a celestial being, or a wizard?" The Buddha answered simply, "I am awake."[4] That's exactly how I felt regaining my spiritual life via this fresh and well-fitting path: totally and completely awake.

Because a parched person craves water, I also was drawn to Bhakti, an ancient devotional worship and spiritual path honoring certain gods or goddesses and different manifestations of the One. Bhakti is still practiced by many Hindus today. When I heard my first call-and-response kirtan chanting concert, led by Grammy Award–nominated singer Jai Uttal, goose bumps overcame me, and the Sanskrit chants touched me so deeply that tears streamed down my cheeks; again, I knew I belonged right there. Uttal describes kirtan as "the calling, the crying, the reaching across infinite space—digging into the heart's deepest well to touch and be touched by the Divine Presence...A power tool of love and longing. A train carrying us home."[5] With kirtan, I learned a new, amazingly powerful way to open my heart to help, and a meaningful way to direct my prayers.

Finally, a three-day shamanic workshop with well-known research scholar and paleoanthropologist Hank Wesselman, PhD stunned me with many layers of indigenous spiritual wisdom. With nine bestselling books on the subject of shamanic healing and spirituality, and a shaman himself, Wesselman taught the 30 of us an appreciation for the rich spirit world, the wisdom and forces of nature, and, essentially, a respect for the power of inner worlds and outer worlds.

My patchwork beliefs of Christianity, Buddhism, Bhakti, and Shamanism seem just right for me, are all with me every day, and serve as a multi-fingered glove that perfectly fits, holds my hand, and ultimately leads me home.

THE *CONNECT TO A HIGHER POWER* SPOKE AND WEALTH-BEING

What did vastly improving my *Connect to a Higher Power* spoke do for me? As seen on the positive personal outcomes ring of the Wealth-Being Wheel, I felt immense elation, the surreal joy that comes with knowing that, deep down, I wasn't struggling all alone after all. Every time I sing a kirtan chant or pray, I remember that I have help and am divinely watched over.

The belief systems that were right for me led me to more self-compassion, love for others, and most of all, a faith that things, as dire as they seemed at the time, were going to work out for my highest good. As I healed, I saw in real time that this was indeed absolutely true. It was so powerful for me to marry my overarching positive attitude with this higher-power aspect. My illnesses, though I would never wish them on anyone, were a gift that altered the course of my life, and they set me up for meaningful service to humanity.

As far as positive professional outcomes on the Wealth-Being Wheel, my *Connect to a Higher Power* spoke, for me, most closely points to peak performance. Because I pray often, be it to God, or Jesus, or, say, the Hindu god Ganesh (who removes obstacles), I feel more empowered. I feel I have a divine team behind me, cheering me on. I feel boosted, like I have an extra advantage.

Over the years, this revived spoke prompted me to ask my executive clients more about their own religious and spiritual belief systems, and interestingly, almost all have a belief in a higher power. I have gained a deeper respect for the wide variety of belief expressions. It opened a closeness between us that was not there before, which is good for relationships and business.

Are you ready to experience this thought-provoking spoke? I am not out to change your beliefs here. This is a very personal subject, but for those interested, let's see if I can help you connect to a higher power even more powerfully.

CUSTOMIZING THE *CONNECT TO A HIGHER POWER* SPOKE FOR YOU

1. How would you define your belief in a higher power? Do you belong to a particular religion? Do you have a spiritual belief? A mixture of beliefs? Do you have a favorite inspirational text? However you define your belief system, I think it's helpful to write it out or think through it for *you*, right now, in the present time.

2. How does this belief in a higher power serve you? How do you benefit? Is it something you use daily, or rarely? You could start with this sentence: My beliefs help me _____.

3. How does your belief system allow you to serve others? So often, we are focused exclusively on ourselves. It's useful to think of how our beliefs might help us be of service—how we might engage to make the world a better place.

4. Is there any aspect of this belief system that is calling you to explore further? If so, start reading articles and books, attend services, take classes, and so forth. Expand your knowledge as well as open your heart.

5. If you don't believe in God or a higher power *per se*, could you cultivate wonder for nature, say a reverence for the ocean or for the animal kingdom? Could you develop an appreciation for something more expansive than yourself? I believe this could help your well-being.

There is really no right or wrong here, just a gentle offering. The aim is for you to reach beyond yourself for meaning—for a sense of belonging to an extended world—and however you do that is a personal experience.

INCREDIBLE WELL-BEING CUSTOMIZATIONS FROM AN EXCEPTIONAL EXECUTIVE

Angela Macke, RN, Founder and Director, Light of Day Organics

Angela Macke explains that tea "is the most labor-intensive agricultural plant known to man."

To produce just one pound of her Light of Day Organics tea, more than 70,000 tea leaves need to be picked by hand, and the entire process, from the drying of the leaves to the finish blending to the onsite packaging, takes four full days. The company produces dozens of fair-trade, award-winning white teas, green teas (like Just Plain Green and Lemon Sencha), oolong teas, daily and ceremonial grade matcha, black teas (like Ceylon Breakfast and Creamy Earl Grey), and tisanes (like Blueberry Blessings) made of botanicals like herbs, spices, and fruit. She admits, "I knew what I was getting into, but it's insane!"

Founded in 2004, Light of Day Organics is a tea company and a fully sustainable, 75-acre farm in Traverse City, Michigan, home to more than 250 botanicals, and it is the only Certified Organic and Certified Demeter Biodynamic commercial grower of tea plants in North America. The University of Michigan has adopted it as their official tea, which means that students on campus as well as patients in the university's hospitals can enjoy it.

Angela has found that not only has she created a thriving business, but also her company, her farming process, and the land itself have provided her with an unexpected and invaluable way to connect with something greater than herself—a higher power. She feels there is sacredness in the land, nature, and all living things. This belief flows into her company's values, and she shares her company tagline: "Sit down, sip your tea, and just appreciate the wonder of every created thing."

Let's start with Angela and her reverence for the land. Although she says that Biodynamic farming likely would have been historically described as pagan, with *bio* meaning *life* and *dynamic* meaning *forces*, at a practical level, it's what she calls "regenerative farming," because it heals the earth and *increases* vitality. Angela and her team follow a lunar calendar to identify the most fertile times to plant and the most ideal times to harvest. She explains, "By paying attention to those naturally occurring rhythms and cycles in nature, we have increased our yield by over thirty percent, just by working with those cycles and rhythms instead of working against them, and the quality has improved every year. For instance, we produce more essential oils yearly from our lavender and our mint. They get stronger and stronger." As an example, she mentions their cacao mint tea: "I used to say you need a teaspoon of tea for eight ounces of water, and now I recommend a teaspoon of tea for sixteen ounces of water. It is so much more minty than it used to be when I first began producing it fifteen years ago."

Also, the farm and the multiple company buildings on the land have all been solar powered since 2008 and use minimal inputs from outside sources. Angela says they have established a "closed loop system" where "everything is from the land here." She cares about soil aeration, homeopathic preparations added to the soil, and even the worm count, which has increased over the years from a measly five worms when she started to her current 200 per five-gallon bucket. She proudly monitors the pounds of carbon the farm takes out of the atmosphere and returns to the soil by creating rich humus. She believes these actions, which are "more than an awareness" and are instead "an adherence," beautifully respect all species—"It's a sanctuary, and all species are welcome."

With a nod to the intense labor of tea production, she laughingly admits, "I could not have bitten off a higher standard," but it's a win-win for the best possible outcome: nutrient-rich soil; increasingly abundant yields; fairly paid, family-like employees who pick with "happy hands" (she says this energy is important); and flavorful and superior organic teas.

Angela Macke is a Specialty Tea Institute graduate, a Green America Partner, and an Advanced Master Gardener and Mentor. She is a tea instructor at her own company and with the Great Lakes Culinary Institute, a holistic licensed RN, a Healing Touch Practitioner, and a nationally recognized speaker.

Before farming, Angela worked extensively in emergency rooms and intensive care units, and interestingly, she was chronically ill herself. For many painful years, she had a severe allergy to wheat that was misdiagnosed as Crohn's disease. Now she feels she "can have much greater impact outside of the hospital walls by teaching prevention and alignment and helping prevent the crisis to begin with." She adds, "It's a unique combination for me of being a nurse, being a farmer, being sick, and getting better. That's how this formula happened."

Besides a sacred connection with the land, Angela treasures her ability to teach guests how to connect to a higher power via "Chado" (the "Way of Tea") in her onsite Tea Wellness class. She grew up Catholic, but she says that because tea is part of every culture around the globe, her offering here is intended to be universal, "neither right nor left," noting that it "doesn't declare any certain religion." She believes we could all define this "way" for ourselves and create a deeply spiritual experience of reverence and mindfulness.

She notes that many cultural rituals mimic "the ceremony of all ceremonies: The Tea Ceremony." Drawing upon Japanese and Chinese traditions, she shares her favorite elements of removing your shoes, ducking down through a low doorway as a gestural symbol of humility, and entering in silence into the sacred space out of reverence, "where everyone is on an equal playing field. It doesn't matter who you are."

An important part of her Tea Ceremony is the forgiveness exercise, where "you let yourself off the hook, and you let your brothers and sisters off the hook. This paves the way for this being a time designated to be closer to the divine."

She loves teaching the process where "each article to be used in the Tea Ceremony is passed around to appreciate the intense human effort." In a practice that she says is akin to "stopping to smell the roses," everything is appreciated, from the painstakingly crafted teacups to the handmade bamboo matcha whisks. But with tea, ultimately, she says, "the sacrifice is the labor of love that went into producing it."

Angela teaches the students to feel the heat of their teacups and to have a multisensory experience rooted in deep appreciation for the teas, which have vast health benefits. She feels that teaching people to support their bodies, minds, and hearts with nutritious content will "give them the strength to do what they are on this earth to do."

Angela explains that because many of us are so busy, so distracted, and so tied to our electronic devices, taking our time to pause in reverence often resonates. She adds, "It's great to see people light up."

According to Angela, if we "make time to listen to the call of spirit," we can wake up and tap into our divine potential. Her best analogy for all of us is, of course, something from nature: a tree. She explains that when we "look up at that canopy and we know beneath us is an almost matching root system, it's like uncaptured human potential. You are seeing an example of the bigness of you and your capacity as a human being."

Angela hopes that she inspires an interconnectedness with nature, with others, and with ourselves. She believes that these deeply resonant forces can lift an ordinary existence to one that is more miraculous. She says, "What I can do with Light of Day is for me the ultimate expression of reverence and respect for life. What has been so unplanned but such a gift is that it has been a platform to talk about these issues that really matter to me. It's the most meaningful work I have ever done."

As she advises everyone attending her tea class, for the best possible experience, "Come with an open heart."

Craft Self-Expression: Igniting Your Inner Muse

"…the world offers itself to your imagination,
calls to you like the wild geese, harsh and exciting—
over and over announcing your place
in the family of things."[1]

—Mary Oliver, "Wild Geese"

A HALF-BAKED CAKE

Before the start of my well-being journey, I had all the makings of a unique, multifaceted individual in my foundation, but only glimmers of it showed at any given time. In terms of self-expression, I was akin to a half-baked cake: almost there, but not quite.

When I started to examine my level of self-expression, I realized that I would only let out certain sides of myself depending on the situation, like opening the oven to let out just a waft of that half-baked cake. I think that I learned this strategy to deal with the broad dichotomies in my life experience. For instance, it's true that I was born in a modest Midwest farm town *and* went to an exclusive boarding school on the East Coast, where I felt conflicted about the fact that I could easily drive a tractor *and* I felt totally comfortable exploring a museum. It's true I graduated with honors in English *and* was successful in my financial career; I could maneuver in conversations about Shakespeare *and* economics, although I didn't reveal that to many clients. It was true that I was a wife (back then), a mom, *and* a career woman. I tried to keep those last three separate, so as not to cloud my concentration and power in whichever area I was focusing on. Can you relate?

I began to realize that it might be hurting my well-being not to be fully, completely myself at all times—to not have an integrated image and reflective surroundings that encompassed all that I am.

How could I be self-expressive in a way that would help my well-being, my personal life, and my professional life? It was a tall order, but at that point, I was on a roll!

STEPPING UP FOR THE *CRAFT SELF-EXPRESSION* SPOKE

Your self-expression can come in many different, creative forms. For example, you could express your unique self with cooking, writing, photography, music, art, crafts, dance, computer design, gardening, stand-up comedy—the list of ways is as vast as there are individuals on this planet. What we are looking for is your personal excitement around a conduit for *your* expression.

I started my *Craft Self-Expression* revamp with two things—my appearance and my home surroundings—and set out to integrate who I really was. I was also in power-healing mode and feeling better by the day, which made this work all the more gratifying for me.

As Julia Cameron, author of *The Artist's Way*, beautifully says, "As we lose our vagueness about ourself, our values, our life situation, we become available to the moment. It is there, in the particular, that we contact the creative self. Art lies in the moment of encounter; we meet our truth and we meet ourselves; we meet ourselves and we meet our self-expression."[2]

Likewise, I set about trying to eliminate vagueness and to define, in the broadest terms possible, who I was. I didn't want to be "this and that" anymore. I wanted to be one thing—truly *me*—something integrated.

Interestingly, *someone else* unexpectedly spelled out a unifying truth for me. At the end of a self-expression workshop, the teacher took me aside and said "Well, it's obvious as day! Your gift is VIBRANCY."

My jaw dropped. Why is it that we sometimes cannot see for ourselves what is so clear to others? Like a bolt of lightning, that word struck me as one of the truest things anyone has ever said about me. I immediately owned it like a badge of honor. As both a child and as an adult, whether I have been in the Midwest, East Coast, the South, or California, no matter what I have been doing, I have always been vibrant.

Because I love the fashion and beauty industries, I started my self-expression revamp with my image, seeking to marry that core quality of vibrancy to how I looked. I wanted who I was and how I presented in the world to match.

Also, I started there because I know the power of first impressions is extremely well-documented. Princeton psychologists Janine Willis and Alexander Todorov, in their notable research study on first impressions, concluded that it takes about one tenth of a second to form an impression of a stranger, as well as to make judgments like trustworthiness, attractiveness, likeability, and competence.[3] In other words, people assess you in no time! I decided to use that basic fact to my advantage and put my best, true self forward at all times.

Amped up with courage, I changed my hair color to red, which fits right in with my Irish heritage, fair skin, green-and-gold eyes, and hundreds of freckles. Then I slowly revamped my mostly dark and navy professional closet. I asked myself, "What would a vibrant professional who manages money for executives wear to work?" I started collecting well-made blazers in all shades of orange, burgundy, and camel, and I found patterned, bright silk shirts and gorgeously detailed, colorful, gemstone jewelry. I always make sure to look polished and professional, usually with one standout, vibrant element. For weekends, these same pieces work perfectly with cargo pants and jeans. I successfully created my new look.

For my actual home, which was my second revamp project, I decided to start fresh by applying my vibrant vibe to my interior design. During our divorce I gave my husband many of the items we had collected together, which left several blank walls. I wanted my home to reflect who *I am* in essence, and the energy of the old memories just didn't feel right. Consequently, the girls and I bought new, vibrant art—both original paintings and colorful photographs. Now the unique trinkets around our home reflect things we love, such as the trays of multicolored stones on display and framed cards from people who cherish us. In a grand final flourish, I repainted my master bedroom metallic gold, and it shimmers when the setting sun hits the walls.

It all takes my breath away—it's so ME.

THE *CRAFT SELF-EXPRESSION* SPOKE AND WEALTH-BEING

This *Craft Self-Expression* spoke started with my desire to fully express myself and to have others see me as I really am, and it has had an unexpectedly profound effect on my life. I had no idea that it would help my well-being and success so much.

As far as positive personal outcomes on the Wealth-Being Wheel, I began walking around with a deep gratitude for who I really am. Truthfully, I always liked and appreciated myself, but actually defining what made me special and different in the world helped me be much happier, because I actually know what sets me apart.

Many of us realize we are amazing, but we haven't taken the time to define exactly *why* that is. It sounds crazy, but believe me, I ask people, *"But what sets you apart? What makes you different?"* and many can't answer it. It's so empowering to know your special version of the vibrancy or uniqueness you bring.

As far as positive professional outcomes, my focus on self-expression has catapulted my business, because every new potential client I meet knows immediately what they are getting. I am being myself. Truly.

Rather than wearing my black suit and trying to be fairly neutral and likeable to every executive I am honored to present to, now I just step out as my vibrant, more interesting self, professional, smiling, and confident. It points on the Wealth-Being Wheel to communication mastery because I am communicating who I am and exactly what I mean to say. Can I tell that I am too vibrant for some prospective clients? Absolutely, but I remind myself that, down the line, our true personalities would have come out anyway, and, as in a long-term relationship, it's much better to be authentic up front. This saves me and my incredible assistants an inordinate amount of time. With my clients, our trust-based relationships last for years, even decades. We really need to understand each other and be in sync.

I would say that on the Wealth-Being Wheel, this also points to visionary thinking. I am thinking about my future vision, and which clients, most powerfully, I can help and impact in a positive way. For all these reasons, I stand out from other typical advisors, and my market superiority and financial freedom have increased. What's not to appreciate about that?

Are you ready to unleash your true self and experience this critical spoke? This is going to be gratifying!

CUSTOMIZING THE *CRAFT SELF-EXPRESSION* SPOKE FOR YOU

1. Consider choosing a core defining word or two to inspire you toward self-expression. Is there a word that describes you, your essence, no matter where you are or what you are doing? Jot down some ideas and see if any jump out at you as something you can own AND feel great about. *Nothing negative!* You are looking for positive, descriptive words like *creative, artsy, serious, thoughtful, peaceful, mellow, loving, reflective, confident,*

outgoing, playful, polished, free-spirited, optimistic, etc. See if you can choose a word that describes you at your best. You get the idea.

2. Now, what would be a favorite form of self-expression for you? I really want to leave this open as the possibilities for you are endless. In what medium could you see your true soul take flight?

3. Now marry that chosen word from step 1 with your chosen form of self-expression from step 2. For instance, if your chosen word is *thoughtful* and your expression is charity work, start using that word as a guide to assess whether you are expressing your innate thoughtfulness with a particular charity. Make sense?

4. Seek ongoing inspiration for your chosen modality. Find inspiration in print or online or in person, whatever your modality. Any time that you have an in-person meeting or group, you never know what inspiration or like-minded souls you might encounter.

5. Find a way to express yourself, even if it means jotting down notes and ideas now and then deciding later. Plant a seed now, and see what grows.

INCREDIBLE WELL-BEING CUSTOMIZATIONS FROM AN EXCEPTIONAL EXECUTIVE

Kim Todd, Owner and General Manager, diPietro Todd Salons & Academy

It's a typical Tuesday in the Jackson Square diPietro Todd Salon in downtown San Francisco, located diagonally across the street from the iconic Transamerica Pyramid. Inside, Kim Todd sits with her laptop and phone in the front part of the hair salon, right in the middle of the busy foray. Kim, who ditched her private back office years ago, straightforwardly explains, "I want them to see me, and I want to be here for them." She looks perfectly at home amidst her busy staff and steady stream of clients.

Her company, diPietro Todd, has been at the forefront of the beauty industry in the San Francisco Bay Area and nationwide for more than 30 years. It employs more than 145 stylists, colorists, and assistants, and it also maintains multiple salons in the high-end districts of the downtown Financial District, Pacific Heights, and the surrounding Bay Area. As consistent yearly winners in *San Francisco Magazine*'s "Best of the Bay" awards, their talent has been featured at New York's Fashion Week and also in *Allure*, *Salon Today*, and *Health Magazine*, to just name a few. The company is a trusted style partner for movers and shakers, luminaries who shift and change modern culture, and tech giants, and even Marc Benioff, founder and CEO of Salesforce, has had his hair cut here for decades.

Kim travels between all of the salons, and each day means a different location. She says they have an inside staff joke that she is "here, there, everywhere, and somewhere." Despite being on the move, as the owner and general manager, she oversees a pattern of weekly meetings in each salon location, including a business meeting that she heads up, a demonstration related to hair that the creative department leads, and education on product knowledge. Rinse and repeat each week, each salon.

She explains, "We are not just a hair salon; we are running a sizeable, serious business." The company manages multiple locations and sells a tremendous amount of hair products. For example, they were the first salon ever to carry Bumble and bumble products, and they are the top distributor nationwide for various brands. Kim coordinates with partners and managers at each location; they host buzz-worthy theme celebrations for their employees, who are like family; and they have a world-class, highly demanding training program for new stylists.

Kim, who cut hair for many years, explains that "the industry I have chosen to dedicate my life to is about selling beauty, helping clients tap into their personal style, and helping them look like the best version of themselves." In that way, Kim's entire company is a professional operation dedicated to the quest for ideal and heightened self-expression.

To that end, she comments that as the providers entrusted to deliver that style and beauty to clients, "*our* image is really important." She consciously uses her unique self-expression, including her image, to set a professional, grounded tone for a highly creative company in a fast-moving industry.

One of the first ways Kim describes herself is "consistent." She explains, "I run my life that way." She loves to express herself through fashion. This includes how she dresses and, as other stylists note, "her fabulous hair!" which is blond, shoulder length, and beautifully styled back off her face.

Even with how casual society has become, Kim, who is polished and professional, downtown glamour meets California with an edge of sexiness, says she loves getting dressed up. "I refuse to dress down. I want to look like the owner. If you look successful, you usually are successful. I want every client who walks in to know that I am someone important here."

Kim has two style icons: Robin Wright's character, Claire Underwood, who plays the president of the United States in the sixth season of *House of Cards*; and Kerry Washington's character, Olivia Pope, in *Scandal*. Both characters wield immense power, dress appropriately for their age, look professional *and* beautiful, wear perfectly fitting clothes with solid colors and clean lines, and have a keen mastery of keeping the sexiness on the side of being taken seriously. Kim admires that, and says she also tries to "get it just right."

To that end, she's also consistent with her look. On a typical day, she might wear a spotless white, ruffled blouse tucked into pressed trousers and stylish high heels. Her body language matches her appearance, and she leans back in a chair with the ease of someone who knows exactly who she is. Recently, she appeared for work in a light-pink silk shirt, matching pants, a blush-colored suede and shearling jacket, and a tan Prada purse. She says she chooses the next day's outfit the night before from her carefully organized closet, a routine that streamlines her morning and makes things easy. Instead of spending time on outfit decisions, Kim focuses on the business of her day ahead.

Kim, who is beautiful enough to be a model herself, believes that her ideal self-expression at work is also fueled by a strongly feminine vibe. She says that alongside her incredible success, deeply feminist values, and penchant for hardcore data collecting to make business decisions, she values what she describes as that "soft-hearted" part of herself. She says, "At the end of the day, you have to respect people. I go to sleep at night knowing that I made good decisions. I want to be in my power, promote equal rights for all people, and at the end of the day, I still want to be a woman."

Kim's consistent approach to her self-expressive appearance translates into her overall flair for consistency in general. She's in bed every night by 9:30, noting "I am exhausted and want to be my best everyday"; she does her most productive work at 5:30 a.m.; and she is never late to the salon. Every Tuesday, she meets with the newest group of assistants, whom she connects with about everything from the company history to the company values, which are discipline, passion, and truth. She says that right off the bat, they get that "I have a high standard. It's always the same. There are no changes. I am a nice lady, I am reasonable, but I do have a high standard."

Interestingly, her consistently professional look and consistent high-standards approach is the perfect container for a wildly creative staff working in a fast-paced environment. Also, Kim proudly notes that her company is dominated by women and minority groups, with a large percentage of leadership roles and top earners who are female, people of color, and members of the LGBTQ+ community. Kim says that many employees appreciate the opportunity-rich, accepting environment, and the chance to work with colleagues who feel like a warm family; this allows them to grow into consummate professionals earning a very good living.

She encourages the entire company to consider their unique self-expression, and to stay current. Luckily, she says, "I am attracted to all kinds of images," and so as long as her employees look like they have put in a conscious effort, she's open and appreciative of interesting hairstyles, imaginative makeup, funky clothes, unique tattoos, rocker looks, chic expressions, and whatever they feel suits their personalities best.

Beyond the images of the staff, each of the open, airy, modern salons is an exercise in self-expression, as they feature huge, bold, and interesting rotating art shows of local talent. Even her charitable work is an exercise in self-expression; she and the salon group have partnered with "Rise Up," an organization that supports girls and women around the world.

Kim lets her own creative side express itself in a different way: in her mélange of personal photographs and shared images on her social media,[4] which show just how open she is to living a self-expressive, art-filled, cultured, and well-travelled life. Photos show her enjoying the Red Hot Chili Peppers with her adult daughter; participating in a shadow yoga retreat at Esalen in Big Sur; exploring a seventeenth-century street in Symi, her favorite island in Greece; experiencing a sound bath with friends at Joshua Tree National Park; seeing cellist Yo-Yo Ma perform at the Greek Theater; and hiking a redwood-lined trail on Mount Tamalpais. Because she also shares countless images of thought-provoking, avant-garde, and even macabre modern art, it's easy to see that she's created a makeshift personal gallery of favorites that have caught her eye or her fancy, and that she truly celebrates both art and self-expression.

Also, amidst the art, there are images of Kim exploring the Tokyo fish market with her handsome husband, love of her live, and business partner of 33 years, Andrew Todd, who is the creative director and co-owner of diPietro Todd. Kim says they "are perfect together," and while he's the consummate creative, she's the "born manager." Dozens of photos on her social media show the couple dressed up in astonishingly detailed costumes for their company's yearly party—from futuristic to Goth—and it's obvious that even their relationship is an expression of a rare and dynamic connection.

Kim believes that there is tremendous personal gratification and undeniable business potential in the ability to master self-expression, because she has firsthand knowledge of its power for herself and for her successful business. As she looks around her buzzing salon, each chair filled with customers getting fresh hairstyles and new color, she smiles and says, very simply, that it's "the ability to know who you are and what you want."

Create Intimacy: Inspiration for Love

"Life is nothing but a dream, and if we are artists,
then we can create our life with Love, and our dream
becomes a masterpiece of art."[1]

—Don Miguel Ruiz

RELATIONSHIP REBOOT

The decision to end my 12-year marriage remains for me a sacred and deeply private determination. Essentially, in 2010 I knew in the core of my being that it was time for us to part ways as married people. I strongly felt, even in those excruciating moments of truth, that this relationship was over, everything happens for a reason, that everything is a co-creation and we all play our part, and that ultimately the parting would improve my well-being. I even saw a door open in my mind's eye; that was a loud, clear message that I needed to follow my heart, and I did.

Fortunately, we never parted as loving *parent* partners for our beautiful girls, who were then ages six and eight. In a conscious pact, we vowed to never speak an ill word about the other to our daughters, ever, and we have continued to honor that promise.

My relationship with my girls was always strong, because I spent considerable time with them, but before our divorce, it had a quality of everyday function more than of deep, heart-based connection. With so much pain in my body, I was just trying to get by. I knew that I could do a better job at being more present, a better job at looking them in the eyes, a better job at listening, and a better job at simply getting to know who they were becoming. Can't we all?

At this same time, I found myself somewhat isolated from most of my friends. The two exceptions were my sister, Mollie, based in New York, whom I spoke to every day via phone, and my longtime, childhood soul friend, Marguerite, based in Tucson. I didn't have many in-person connections to lean on other than work friends, and I felt lonely. Where was my tribe? I could have used one right about then.

I knew that my relationships needed a reboot—perhaps a shutdown and restart! The simple awareness that there was room for improvement was a blessing, and I set about on a quest to enhance my close connections, the relationships that make life worth living.

EMBRACING THE *CREATE INTIMACY* SPOKE

With my intention for more closeness in my life, the *Create Intimacy* spoke was born. I focused on intimacy as it related to three areas: my future partner, my girls, and my friends.

As a way to heal from my divorce, I began to create a new, fresh vision of what ideal romantic love would look like for me someday. I felt crystal clear that even though I was ending an important relationship, I was moving *toward* love, greater love for myself and, hopefully, a greater love from a future partner.

I began to read everything I could on the topic of love. It was a book club for one for the next two years, and it was one of the most gratifying projects I've ever done.

I read dozens of books, but a few stand out. I devoured Matthew Kelly's *The Seven Levels of Intimacy: The Art of Loving and the Joy of Being*

Loved, appreciating how he describes that the purpose of a relationship is to help each other become the best versions of ourselves. I took six pages of notes, which I still have. I also highlighted how "important it is to involve ourselves with people who have thought about life, who have a sense of who they are and what they want, and people who know their values, and know how to own them in a real and personal way."[2] Yes!

My friend Kee-Ann, who gave me Kelly's book, added her own mantra, which I adopted: "Love fearlessly as though there's no such thing as a broken heart." Many of us can relate to that.

I read Gary Chapman's *New York Times* bestseller *The 5 Love Languages*, and I learned that tailoring your appreciation to your partner's communication style positively amplifies its effect—whether it's words of affirmation, quality time, gifts, acts of service, or physical touch.[3] How good to know! Interestingly, all of those matter to me.

Don Miguel Ruiz's *The Mastery of Love*, contains many truths, especially about the importance of self-acceptance, and I love his overarching teaching that "if you have the eyes of love, you just see love wherever you go."[4] I also agree that "when you become wise, your life is controlled by your heart, not your head."[5]

I collected dozens of articles on love and I even created a special folder to hold them. I eventually healed enough to venture toward new, real-life, meaningful connections.

Overall, I learned that for me, an extraordinary partner relationship would be based on three things: outstanding physical chemistry, excellent communication, and deeply shared values. All three of those elements need to be in place, or I am not interested. At this point in my life, *extraordinary* interests me.

My daughters, who are now teenagers, and I have developed a sacred bond beyond anything I could properly describe here, but I can say that they love me as much as I love them. After my divorce, I began to be more deliberate, calm, and conscious of what we were creating together. They expressed passion about music, theater, and art, and as a trio (or as duos on our yearly mother–daughter trips where I take each separately), we have been to everything from Christmas soirees to classical solo flute concerts, Broadway shows, museum exhibitions, international gem shows, and modern art galleries.

As I mentioned, my time with my girls was lively and engaging, but my newfound time alone, when they were with their dad, was stark, silent, and lonely by comparison. I suddenly realized that although I knew hundreds of people, I didn't have that many close friends in my area. Can you relate? I asked myself, "How can I create an authentic group of friends?"

I came upon a bold, risky, and fun idea to remedy that. I had always loved the legendary stories of literary giant Gertrude Stein having *salons* at her Left Bank home in Paris in the 1920s, hosting luminaries like Fitzgerald and Hemingway for sparkling conversation. I decided to start a modern in-person salon series at my home, set about creating a theme for each one, and invited anyone I thought might enjoy it, including some clients and my assistants.

Although I was terrified no one would come, 25 people showed up the first night, and my salons turned into a series. During these gatherings, we'd crowd into my living room, balancing our wine and hors d'oeuvres on our laps. I loved every minute. Different nights featured a jazz trumpeter, an exotic animal specialist, and an acclaimed travel writer, among others. One of the salons occurred on my actual birthday, no entertainment was needed, and there I was, finally celebrating among friends.

THE *CREATE INTIMACY* SPOKE AND WEALTH-BEING

This *Create Intimacy* spoke requires taking a risk to see others, to engage them, and to get to know them. Simultaneously, it requires being willing to be seen in a deep, authentic way. It's a two-way street.

In a Massachusetts gift shop, I bought a golden metallic sign, smaller than a postcard, engraved with the words "Open Heart." It's still hanging on my bedroom wall. To experience intimacy—whether with a partner, with family, or with friends—you need an open heart.

As far as positive personal outcomes, as you can see right across from this spoke on the Wealth-Being Wheel, I began to experience more deep connection with the people around me. I was deeply engaged, taking time to stop and to learn something about them. When you have chronic pain, it can make you go inward, and this conscious connecting caused an outward reset. It was healing.

As far as positive professional outcomes on the Wealth-Being Wheel, my *Create Intimacy* spoke really boosted my communication mastery. Creating intimacy in a business setting with clients involves creating a bond of mutual respect where they trust you and they feel understood. As the service provider, I believe that it isn't so important that they know details about *my* life as it is that I truly grasp theirs. When you actively listen to and understand your clients, you can serve them better. With valuable information, you can communicate exactly how you might provide yet another outcome, impeccable service, a win-win for everyone. Since I upped my game on this, I have had clients invite me to their son's Eagle Scout inductions, to shopping excursions in Sonoma, to holiday parties, to backyard Easter get-togethers, and to spiritual wisdom conferences, and I tremendously value our growing connections. I adore them.

Are you ready to open up your heart and experience this meaningful spoke? Of course you are!

CUSTOMIZING THE *CREATE INTIMACY* SPOKE FOR YOU

1. When you are with someone, you want to deepen your bond: be with them, listen to them, and seek to learn something about them. It's an outward focus, where you concentrate on *them* with your deep, caring nature.
2. I mentioned this in the *Intuition* spoke, but it's helpful here as well: try to look people in the eyes more at home and at work. I feel this is a lost art, yet an incredible communication channel,

with an inordinate amount of clues that will help you connect and build intimacy.

3. Continue to practice loving yourself. I believe that the amount you can love others is in direct proportion to how much you love and accept yourself. How might you do this? Create a list of everything positive about yourself that you can think of. Refer to it often. Beware of negative self-talk. Speak to yourself as if you are speaking to a best friend.

4. If you are in a relationship, figure out the way that your significant other likes to be appreciated: with words, actions, touch, or gifts. It can have an exponentially positive effect when you connect in *your partner's* favorite way.

5. Spend time with the people you love. Time is the most precious commodity we have, and the most precious gift we can give a loved one.

6. If you are eager to build a friend tribe, do things you enjoy doing where there are other people doing that same thing. If you love hiking, join a hiking group. If you love to read, join a local book club. Meetup.com is a great resource for connecting with other like-minded souls.

INCREDIBLE WELL-BEING CUSTOMIZATIONS FROM AN EXCEPTIONAL EXECUTIVE

Scott Kucirek, Cofounder and CEO, OCHO Candy; Serial Entrepreneur

When Scott Kucirek was just out of the United States Navy's flight training program and newly assigned to his squadron, he spoke with a chief about someone who had retired from the Navy after 30 successful working years. The retired man had sacrificed everything personal for the Navy, and when he left, he went back to no family, no home, and no friends. Then, perhaps since his whole life had been the Navy and his work, he died not more than a year later. Considering it a cautionary tale, the chief advised Scott, who was 24 years old at the time, that "the Navy will go on. If you die tomorrow, or you leave, you will be replaced. So make sure that you don't put that as your priority. Put your family and your friends as your priority, because those are the people who will be with you no matter what."

That one pivotal conversation, which Scott has never forgotten, steered him toward a life centered around meaningful relationships. In 2018, he celebrated his twenty-fifth wedding anniversary with his wife, Mirjana, a skilled psychologist and loving soul. They have a noticeable ease, a deep respect, a playful familiarity, and a team spirit that is authentic and rare.

Scott explains, "I value her as someone so important in my life. I am not perfect at this, but I am always working on thanking her, acknowledging her, taking time out to do things with her, and having fun together." Empty nesters after their second daughter started her freshman year at UCLA, he says, "We are just back to where we were before we had kids! We are just rediscovering how much we love each other."

Spending time together is a top priority. They spend Tuesday evenings in Alameda, California, a coastal town near their home, where the movies are a cheap $5.50 a ticket. ("We're frugal," he comments.) They walk the dog every day together, and when Mirjana plans sewing projects, he goes with her to help pick out the fabric. They love traveling worldwide, and since Mirjana is Croatian, they have traveled to Croatia many times. Recently, for his birthday, she took him for a weekend getaway to Mendocino, a stunning oceanfront enclave.

Day to day, Scott thinks it's critical to have dinner together, and they shift their busy schedules to make that happen. Interestingly, he does something notable before he even gets to the table. When he is ready to come home from work, he says, "I am really conscious to check out of work mode and compartmentalize and move to relationship mode. I use that time driving back to make an effort—I don't get three more work conference calls in—it's 'let's just think now, let's switch my brain and think about what's going on with my wife: What is she doing? What should I be asking about, or waiting to hear about?' "

Scott explains that he looks forward to checking in with her: "It's important to me, and it's something I enjoy doing." He describes his time with Mirjana, who is incredibly supportive of his life's work and vision, as a welcome break for him.

He adds that in the evening, "I don't need to talk about work anymore. I talk about that all day. In the end, you need time away, and it makes you a better leader."

Scott remembers a time when he didn't have this coming-from-work, switch-to-relationship focus down pat. He was preparing to graduate with his MBA from the Haas School of Business at the University of California Berkeley and negotiating venture capital funding for his first startup, zipRealty, Inc. a customer-focused, high-tech real estate brokerage. He and his business partner were the first MBA students at the Haas School of Business ever to be funded by a major venture capital firm before completing their studies. When he graduated, the rocketing new company, naturally, consumed much of his attention.

During Scott's startup years, and when his daughters were very young, he'd ask a question at dinner but not listen to the answer. He remembers Mirjana telling him, "You're just not here." Instead of being defensive, he moved toward her, and he was grateful for the feedback, recognizing now that "luckily, she's honest enough to be frank with me!" He thinks these respectful course corrections made all the difference in their closeness over time, and he learned how to become more and more engaged. Scott says that one of the secrets to their success is their ability to be honest with each other, and moreover, respectful of the person and the advice. He says, "Sometimes you need that direct feedback." He adds, "Bottom line, I trust Mirjana completely."

Scott adds that even when we feel pulled in all directions by our careers and other responsibilities, we "*do* have time [to create intimacy], even if it is a little bit. You can make it count."

Since 2010, Scott has been a cofounder, a managing partner, and the CEO of his second major entrepreneurial venture, OCHO Candy, Inc., which makes a line of organic candy bars (*O* stands for *organic* and *CHO* stands for *chocolate*). He runs the day-to-day operations, overseeing manufacturing, sales, business planning, finance, and marketing. His Oakland factory churns out chocolate 24 hours a day to keep up with demand, and their products can be found at Whole Foods, Target, Safeway, Albertsons, and many other places nationwide.

Throughout his business endeavors, Scott has been a consistently present father. Both of his daughters are accomplished students and musicians, and now Juliet is at UCLA and Natalie is in medical school at UCSF. His parenting advice? He says, "The number-one thing you can do is be present in the activities and interests of your child. Not what *you* are interested in but what *they* are interested in."

Case in point: both his daughters were interested in soccer in middle school, and although Scott never played soccer growing up, he jumped at the chance to participate with them and became their long-time coach.

At the time, Scott was acting as the general manager of Prudential California and Nevada Realty—the fourth largest Prudential in the United States at that time—where he oversaw the operations of 2,100 real estate agents in 47 offices with more than $8 billion in real estate sales. His time with his daughters was so important to him, he wrote into his employment contract that he would be unreachable at coaching times and on the weekends when there were soccer games. He told them, "These things are important to me, and I can't *not* do them. If that doesn't work for you, then I can't work here."

Prudential considered Scott's stellar reputation in the field, his successful IPO and exit, and the opportunity to have him on board, and they hired him on his terms. He did an amazing job, and as for his prioritized schedule, he says "they didn't even notice."

His daughters are still on top of his mind, so even though they are both away at their respective universities, he often calls to touch base, "hear the funny snippets," and check in. He says, "I am aware of what they care about." His adds that his daughter in Los Angeles knows that anytime she wants to come home, "she just has to text and she'll have an airline ticket waiting for her." His other daughter is nearby enough to come home for the big games between their alma mater, Berkeley, and

Stanford, the big rivals. Scott's reaction to her desire to attend? "Great, let's go do that!"

Scott also makes time for his friends, a challenging but important task given his considerable time spent with his wife and daughters. He explains, "I like hanging out with interesting, fun people who aren't in my work world, especially people younger than me because I am getting older, and it's about being engaged, talking, taking an interest in other people, and putting yourself out there. I am very comfortable doing that, and I don't mind getting rejected! Over time, I have learned that people are happy to talk with you, especially about what's going on in their lives."

He enjoys jumpstarting activities, being the entrepreneur that he is, and he comments that "I have found that it only takes one person to say, 'Let's do this!' and although others may be overcome with inertia, eventually people will participate and have a great time."

For example, five years ago, for his CrossFit gym, which is one of three affiliates, Scott came up with the idea to do a three-part workout, all on the same day, one at each gym. Convinced it was a fun, engaging group idea, he badgered the owners for weeks, until they reluctantly capitulated and let him put the self-named "Triple Crown" on the calendar. They warned him that if no one signed up, he'd be doing it all alone.

The first year, there were 20 teams of three, and now, in the fifth year, there are more than 30. Fueled with success, Scott dug up an old soccer trophy that looks like a gaudy goblet for the prize, got a friend to deliver pizzas, and asked another to deliver beer. Now the Triple Crown has become one of the favorite yearly events at the gyms.

As we've seen, Scott's personal commitment to relationships began back in his early twenties, without a single business win under his belt, but even now, with all his multiple successes and companies, his stellar reputation, and the fact that he is one of the most sought-after lecturers for business schools, he still feels exactly the same way about meaningful connections. He's carried this priority all along, and it hasn't stopped his personal or professional momentum one bit. In fact, it has enhanced it.

For Scott, and for all of us, a commitment to what makes life worth living, no doubt, makes life worth living.

CONCLUSION: PUTTING IT ALL TOGETHER IN YOUR UP-LEVELED LIFE

"Life calls not for perfection, but for completeness."[1]

—Carl Jung

Together, we have been on a remarkable journey, a heroic quest of the highest order. Let's review the three truths laid out at the start.

Truth #1: TOTAL WELL-BEING is the most valuable asset you have. You now know that to really embody total well-being, the ideal is to embrace a full-circle BODY, MIND, and SPIRIT approach, leaving no aspect of your glorious self behind, knowing you are worth the effort. Your true power comes from this foundation, and you are listening for that click of completeness, when everything locks into place.

Truth #2: Well-being DRIVES success, and because of that Well-Being = Wealth-Being. This is a life-changing belief. You can DO WELL and BE WELL simultaneously, each and every day. Knowing how and why well-being drives success provides motivation for you to strive for the inspirational personal and professional outcomes of wealth-being. My own story is living proof. Extraordinary results are within your reach, waiting for you to claim them.

Truth #3: The most impressive leaders in the world are powered by Well-Being and Wealth-Being. I admire each of our 18 Exceptional Executives; for certain, their stories and examples can be the ultimate inspiration for our own customizations, and they represent a new generation of executives and entrepreneurs who leverage well-being in order to reach their highest potential. I believe that by shining a spotlight on their behind-the-scenes wellness strategies, and showing the undeniable correlation to their proven, continually rising excellence, I have helped ensure that the business world will take notice. There's no going back.

We have indeed "reinvented the wheel."

Well-being is a carefully crafted, inspired way of life.

Well-being, masterfully executed behind the scenes, in your off-time, leads to your greatest health, maximum joy, deepest meaning, and highest potential.

And YOU matter immensely. By your example, you create a ripple effect more powerful than you know, in your family, among your friends, and in your workplace. Most importantly, you accelerate toward all you were meant to be.

ENDNOTES

Introduction: Jumpstart

1. Donald Gordon Carty and Charles F. Haanel, *The Master Key System: Open the Secret to Health, Wealth and Love, 24 Lesson Workbook,* 2nd ed. (Morrisville, NC: Lulu Press, Inc., 2013) 199, Kindle.
2. Dan Lyons, "In Silicon Valley, Working 9 to 5 Is for Losers," *New York Times,* August 31, 2017, Opinion.
3. "Work Related Stress Depression or Anxiety Statistics in Great Britain, 2018," Health and Safety Executive, Government United Kingdom, October 31, 2018, http://www.hse.gov.uk/statistics/causdis/stress.pdf.
4. Michele Hellebuyck, Theresa Nguyen, Madeline Halphern, Danielle Fritze, and Jessica Kennedy, "Mind the Workplace," *Mental Health America,* 2017, http://www.mentalhealthamerica.net/workplace-mental-health.
5. Mayo Clinic Staff, "Chronic Stress Puts Your Health at Risk," Healthy Lifestyle, *Mayo Clinic,* April 21, 2016, https://www.mayoclinic.org/healthy-lifestyle/stress-management/in-depth/stress/art-20046037.
6. "Stress at Work," The National Institute for Occupational Safety and Health, Centers for Disease Control, accessed January 5, 2019, https://www.cdc.gov/niosh/topics/stress/default.html.
7. "High Blood Pressure," Centers for Disease Control and Prevention, November 14, 2018, https://www.cdc.gov/bloodpressure/index.htm.
8. "How Many Americans Have an Autoimmune Disease?" American Autoimmune Related Diseases Association, Inc., April 29, 2017, https://www.aarda.org/knowledge-base/many-americans-autoimmune-disease/.
9. Warren Buffett, interview by Forbes, Forbes, 2017, https://www.forbes.com/100-greatest-business-minds/person/warren-buffett.

Spoke 1—Eat a Healthy, Plant-Centric Diet: Rainbow Food on Planes

1. Dr. Mark Hyman, Dr. Mark Hyman Homepage, last modified February 7, 2019, https://drhyman.com/.

2. Andrew Weil MD, "What Is The Anti-Inflammatory Diet And Food Pyramid?" last modified February 7, 2019, https://www.drweil.com/diet -nutrition/anti-inflammatory-diet-pyramid/what-is-dr-weils-anti -inflammatory-food-pyramid/.
3. Weil, "What Is the Anti-Inflammatory Diet and Food Pyramid?"
4. Weil, "What Is the Anti-Inflammatory Diet and Food Pyramid?"
5. Joel Fuhrman, MD, *Super Immunity: The Essential Nutrition Guide for Boosting Your Body's Defenses to Live Longer, Stronger, and Disease Free* (New York: HarperCollins, 2011), 82.
6. Fuhrman, *Super Immunity*, 122.
7. Leigh Erin Connealy, MD, *The Cancer Revolution: A Groundbreaking Program to Reverse and Prevent Cancer* (Boston: De Capo Press, 2017), iBooks version, 113.
8. Weil, "What Is the Anti-Inflammatory Diet and Food Pyramid?"
9. John Mackey, Alona Puldi, and Matthew Lederman, *The Whole Foods Diet: The Lifesaving Plan for Health and Longevity* (New York: Hachette Book Group, 2017).

Spoke 2—Get Enough Sleep: It's Not Just the Room Temperature

1. Fraser McAlpine, "25 Irish Sayings to Live By," accessed February 10, 2019, http://www.bbcamerica.com/anglophenia/2015/03/25-irish-sayings -to-live-by.
2. Amanda MacMillan, "9 Things to Do When You Can't Sleep Because Your Mind Is Racing," Health.com online, accessed January 26, 2019, https:// www.health.com/sleep/how-to-shut-off-brain-sleep.
3. National Heart, Lung, and Blood Institute, "Sleep Deprivation and Deficiency: How Much Sleep Is Enough?" US Department of Health and Human Services, accessed January 26, 2019, https://www.nhlbi.nih.gov/ health-topics/sleep-deprivation-and-deficiency.
4. National Heart, Lung and Blood Institute, "Sleep Deprivation."
5. Diana Rodriguez (medically reviewed by Pat Bass III, MD, MPH), "Why Alcohol Disrupts Your Sleep," *Everyday Health*, July 9, 2013, https://www .everydayhealth.com/sleep/why-alcohol-disrupts-your-sleep.aspx.
6. Arianna Huffington, "How to Succeed? Get More Sleep," TED Women 2010, https://www.ted.com/talks/arianna_huffington_how_to_succeed_get _more_sleep#t-67996.

7. Arianna Huffington, "Sleep Resources," accessed February 10, 2019, http://ariannahuffington.com/sleep-resources.

8. Denise Brosseau, *Ready to be a Thought Leader? How to Increase Your Influence, Impact, and Success* (San Francisco: Jossey-Bass/Wiley, 2013).

9. Denise Brosseau, "Becoming a Thought Leader," Linkedin.com, https://www.linkedin.com/learning/instructors/denise-brosseau.

10. Susan Pierce Thompson, Ph.D., *Bright Line Eating: The Science of Living Happy, Thin and Free* (Carlsbad, CA: Hay House Publishing, 2017).

11. Matthew Walker, PhD, *Why We Sleep: Unlocking the Power for Sleep and Dreams* (New York: Simon & Schuster, 2017).

Spoke 3—Do Enlivening Exercise: From Net Sports to Nunchucks

1. Rich Roll, "5 Tips for Turning Inspiration into Action," Rich Roll, May 1, 2012, https://www.richroll.com/blog/tips-for-turning-inspiration-into-action/.

2. Edward R. Laskowski, MD, "How Much Should the Average Adult Exercise Every Day?" Mayo Clinic, accessed February 11, 2019, https://www.mayo-clinic.org/healthy-lifestyle/fitness/expert-answers/exercise/faq-20057916.

3. Camille Noe Pagán, "Working Out Through Pain," Arthritis Foundation, https://www.arthritis.org/living-with-arthritis/exercise/how-to/exercise-pain.php.

4. Adeel Safdar et al., "Endurance Exercise Rescues Progeroid Aging and Induces Systemic Mitochondrial Rejuvenation in mtDNA Mutator Mice," *Proc National Academy of Science USA* 108, no. 10 (March 8, 2011): 4135–4140.

5. Mandy Oaklander, "The New Science of Exercise," *Time*, September 12, 2016, http://time.com/4475628/the-new-science-of-exercise/.

6. "P90X Extreme Home Fitness," https://www.beachbody.com/product/fitness_programs/p90x.do.

Spoke 4—Upgrade Your Products: The Health on the Shelf

1. Albert Einstein to Lina Kocherthaler, July 27, 1951, quoted in Jamie Sayen, *Einstein in America: The Scientist's Conscience in the Age of Hitler and Hiroshima* (New York: Crown, 1985), 231.

2. Daniela Ginta (medically reviewed by Debra Rose Wilson, PhD, MSN, RN, IBCLC, AHN-BC, CHT), "Should You Be Going Sulfate Free?" *Healthline*, March 22, 2017, https://www.healthline.com/health/beauty-skin-care/sulfates.

3. Ginta, "Should You Be Going Sulfate Free?"

4. Roddy Scheer and Doug Moss, "Should People Be Concerned about Parabens in Beauty Products?" *Scientific American: Earthtalk*, accessed January 13, 2019, https://www.scientificamerican.com/article/should-people-be-concerned-about-parabens-in-beauty-products/.

5. Scheer and Moss, "Should People Be Concerned about Parabens in Beauty Products?"

6. "Propylene Glycol," EWG's Skin Deep Cosmetics Database, Environmental Working Group, accessed January 13, 2019, http://www.ewg.org/skindeep/ingredient/705315/PROPYLENE_GLYCOL/.

7. Rebekah Edwards, "Propylene Glycol: The Complicated Additive with Potentially Dangerous Side Effects," September 23, 2016, https://draxe.com/propylene-glycol/.

8. "The Never List," Beauty Counter, accessed January 13, 2019, https://www.beautycounter.com/the-never-list.

9. Kris Carr, "Natural Deodorant Review & Tips," accessed January 13, 2019, https://kriscarr.com/blog/kris-carr-natural-deodorant-smackdown/.

10. Kris Carr, "The Best Non-Toxic Nail Polishes," accessed January 13, 2019, https://kriscarr.com/blog/best-non-toxic-nail-polish-review/.

11. "Top Green Cleaning Products," Environmental Working Group, accessed January 13, 2019, http://www.ewg.org/guides/cleaners/content/top_products.

12. "The Never List," Beauty Counter.

13. Environmental Working Group, www.ewg.org.

14. Kris Carr, www.kriscarr.com.

15. May Lindstrom Skin, www.maylindstrom.com.

Spoke 5—Hydrate: Hydration Station

1. L. Pfister, H. H. G. Savenije, and F. Fenicia, *Leonardo Da Vinci's Water Theory: On the Origin and Fate of Water* (Wallingford, UK: International Association of Hydrological Sciences, 2009), vii.

2. "The Importance of Staying Hydrated," *Harvard Health Letter*, June 18, 2015, https://www.health.harvard.edu/staying-healthy/the-importance-of-staying-hydrated.

3. "The Importance of Staying Hydrated."

4. Perricone MD, "The Importance of Hydration for Body and Skin," *Forever Young by Perricone MD Wellness Guide*, https://foreveryoung.perriconemd.com/the-importance-of-hydration-for-body-and-skin.html.

5. Kristeen Cherney (medically reviewed by Kelly Kennedy, RD), "10 Potential Health Benefits of Green Tea Backed by Science," October 8, 2018, https://www.everydayhealth.com/diet-and-nutrition-pictures/life-sustaining-reasons-to-drink-green-tea.aspx#green-tea-may-help-reduce-rheumatoid-arthritis-symptoms.

Spoke 6—Relax: Taking It (Very) Easy

1. Maya Angelou, *Wouldn't Take Nothing for My Journey Now* (New York: Random House, 1993), i.
2. Barton Goldsmith, PhD, "The Importance of Allowing Yourself to Relax: For the Love of a Lazy Sunday," *Emotional Fitness, Psychology Today*, November 20, 2013, https://www.psychologytoday.com/us/blog/emotional-fitness/201311/the-importance-allowing-yourself-relax.
3. Mayo Clinic Staff, "Healthy Lifestyle: Stress Management," Mayo Clinic, last modified Jan 13, 2019, https://www.mayoclinic.org/healthy-lifestyle/stress-management/in-depth/relaxation-technique/art-20045368.
4. Herodotus, *The Histories*, translated by Robin Waterfield (Oxford: Oxford World's Classics, 1998), Book 2, Chapter 173.
5. Yanik Silver, *The Evolved Enterprise: An Illustrated Guide to Re-Think, Re-Imagine, and Re-Invent Your Business to Deliver Meaningful Impact & Even Greater Profits* (Washington, DC: IdeaPress Publishing, 2015).

Spoke 7—Meditate: For the Mind that Veers Between Om and Oops!

1. Ram Dass, "Ram Dass – Here and Now – Ep. 135 – Creation, Creativity and Spirituality," October 19, 2018, https://www.ramdass.org/ram-dass-here-and-now-ep-135-creation-creativity-and-spirituality/.
2. Jack Kornfield, *A Path With Heart: A Guide through the Perils and Promises of Spiritual Life* (New York: Bantam Books, 1993).
3. John Kabat-Zinn, *Full Catastrophe Living: Using the Wisdom of Your Body & Mind to Face Stress, Pain & Illness* (New York: Bantam Dell, 2009).

Spoke 8—Deal with Your "Baggage": Stopping Runaway Roller Coasters

1. Coleman Barks, translations, *The Illuminated Rumi* (New York: Bantam Doubleday Dell Publishing, 1997), 24.

2. Ann Beattie, "Snow," in *Where You'll Find Me: And Other Stories* (New York: Scribner, 2002).
3. Barks, 26.
4. Louise Hay, *You Can Heal Your Life* (Carlsbad, CA: Hay House, Inc., 2004), xiii.
5. Hay, 5.
6. Hay, 4.
7. The Tapping Solution, https://www.thetappingsolution.com/.

Spoke 9—Align Values and Actions: The Proof in the Pudding

1. *Brihadaranyaka Upanishad*, IV, 4.5.
2. Dalai Lama, "Closing Address by His Holiness the Dalai Lama to the Global Buddhist Congregation 2011," New Delhi, India, November 30, 2011, His Holiness the 14th Dalai Lama of Tibet, https://www.dalailama .com/messages/buddhism/buddhist-congregation-2011-address.
3. Adam Fridman. "Four Essential Habits to Align Purpose and Values with Actions," *Inc.com*, June 15, 2017, https://www.inc.com/adam-fridman/ four-essential-habits-to-align-purpose-and-values-with-actions.html.
4. Tony Jeary, "Do Your Actions Reflect Your Values?" *Success.com*, September 19, 2016, https://www.success.com/do-your-actions-reflect-your-values/.
5. Charissa Bradstreet, Chris Ernst, and Steven Rice, "Innovative Practices for Leading Culture," Bill & Melinda Gates Foundation, November 2017, https:// docs.gatesfoundation.org/Documents/innovative_practices_for_leading _culture_09oct17.pdf?lipi=urn%3Ali%3Apage%3Ad_flagship3_pulse_rea d%3BmSiSbyzmS7iITWWaSJMm1Q%3D%3D.
6. Bradstreet, Ernst, and Rice, 11.
7. Bill & Melinda Gates Foundation, Home page, accessed February 10, 2019, https://www.gatesfoundation.org/.

Spoke 10—Speak Your Truth: Just Deliver It with Grace

1. Jackie Strause, "Golden Globes: Oprah Calls for Day When Women Never Have to Say 'Me Too' Again," *Hollywood Reporter*, January 7, 2018, https://www.hollywoodreporter.com/news/oprah-winfrey-golden-globes -2018-speech-1072351.
2. "Guide to Bay Sailing," *Latitude 38*, volume 383, May 2008, 114.

3. Iyanla Vansant, *In the Meantime: Finding Yourself and the Love You Want* (New York: Simon and Schuster, 2012), 114.
4. Judy Belk, "Memories of a Thirsty Childhood," *Los Angeles Times*, August 16, 2015, Op-Ed: Opinion.
5. Judy Belk, "Black Man's Burden," *Los Angeles Times*, January 16, 2011, Archives, http://articles.latimes.com/2011/jan/16/opinion/la-oe-belk-black-men-20110116.

Spoke 11—Hone Your Focus: Zoning in like a Laser

1. Napoleon Hill, *Napoleon Hill's Positive Action Plan: 365 Meditations for Making Each Day a Success* (London: Penguin, 1997), 115.
2. Esther and Jerry Hicks, *The Law of Attraction: The Basics of the Teachings of Abraham* (Carlsbad, CA: Hay House Publishing, 2006).
3. Rhonda Byrne, *The Secret* (New York: Atria Books/Beyond Words, 2006).
4. Hicks and Hicks, *The Law of Attraction*, 24.
5. Jennice Vilhauer PhD, "3 Effective Visualization Techniques to Change Your Life," *Living Forward, Psychology Today*, June 30, 2018, https://www.psychologytoday.com/us/blog/living-forward/201806/3-effective-visualization-techniques-change-your-life.
6. Vilhauer.
7. Hicks and Hicks, *The Law of Attraction*.
8. Esther Hicks and Jerry Hicks, *The Vortex: Where the Law of Attraction Assembles All Cooperative Relationships* (Carlsbad, CA: Hay House, Inc., 2009).
9. Byrnes, *The Secret*.
10. Bruce H. Lipton, *The Biology of Belief: Unleashing the Power of Consciousness, Matter and Miracles* (Carlsbad, CA: Hay House, Inc., 2016).
11. Martin L. Rossman, MD, *Guided Imagery for Self-Healing* (Belvedere, CA: H. J. Kramer/New World Library, 2000).

Spoke 12—Master a Positive Attitude: Here Comes the Sun

1. "Blessed Are the Weird People," Jacob Nordby, March 12, 2015, http://jacobnordby.tumblr.com/post/113471886951/we-wait-starving-for-moment-of-high-magic-to.

2. "Gonna Fly Now," *Theme from Rocky*, performed by Bill Conti et al., Alfred Music, 1979.

3. Barbara L. Frederickson, "The Broaden-and-Build Theory of Positive Emotions," The Royal Society, August 17, 2004, https://www.ncbi.nlm.nih .gov/pmc/articles/PMC1693418/pdf/15347528.pdf.

4. Jane Brody, "A Positive Outlook May Be Good for Your Health," *New York Times*, March 27, 2017, https://www.nytimes.com/2017/03/27/well/live/ positive-thinking-may-improve-health-and-extend-life.html.

5. J.T. Moskowitz et al., "Randomized Controlled Trial of a Positive Affect Intervention to Reduce Stress in People Newly Diagnosed with HIV; Protocol and Design for the IRISS Study," *Open Access Journal of Clinical Trials*, volume 2014:6, September 22, 2014, https://www.dovepress.com/ randomized-controlled-trial-of-a-positive-affect-intervention-to-reduc -peer-reviewed-article-OAJCT.

6. Gopi Kallayil, *The Happy Human: Being Real in an Artificially Intelligent World* (Carlsbad, CA: Hay House Publishing, 2018).

Spoke 13—Develop Intuition: From Passing Illusions to Illustrative Insights

1. Steve Jobs, Commencement Address, *Stanford News*, June 14, 2005, https:// news.stanford.edu/2005/06/14/jobs-061505/.

2. Sonia Choquette, *The Psychic Pathway: A Workbook of Reawakening the Voice of Your Soul* (New York: Harmony, 2015), 14.

3. Choquette, 27.

4. Laura Day, *Practical Intuition: How to Harness the Power of Your Instinct and Make It Work for You* (New York: Villard, 1996).

5. Hrund Gunnsteinsdottir and Kristin Olafsdottir, *InnSaei: The Power of Intuition* (Zeitgeist Films, 2017).

6. Gunnsteindottir and Olafsdottir.

7. Bill Bennett, *PGS—Intuition Is Your Personal Guidance System* (2018), https://www.pgsthemovie.com/.

8. Bennett.

9. Bennett.

10. Bennett.

11. Jen Groover, *What If? & Why Not? How to Transform Your Fears Into Action and Start the Business of Your Dreams* (Dallas: BenBella Books, Inc., 2009).

Spoke 14—Savor Spirit-Lifting Hobbies: Getting in the Flow

1. Elizabeth Gilbert, *Big Magic: Creative Living Beyond Fear* (New York: Riverhead Books/Penguin Random House, 2015), 273.
2. Matthew Zawadzki, Joshua M. Smyth, and Heather J. Costigan, "Real-Time Associations Between Engaging in Leisure and Daily Health and Well-Being," *Annals of Behavioral Medicine* 49, no. 4 (February 2015): 605–615.
3. Xinyi (Lisa) Qian, Careen M. Yarnal, and David M. Almeida, "Does Leisure Time as a Stress Coping Resource Increase Affective Complexity? Applying the Dynamic Model of Affect (DMA)," *Journal of Leisure Research* 45, no. 3 (2013).
4. Mihaly Csikszentmihalyi, *Flow: The Psychology of Optimal Experience* (New York: Harper Collins, 1990), 3.
5. Csikszentmihalyi, 4.
6. Csikszentmihalyi, 3.
7. Riley Etheridge, Jr., *Things I Used to Know* (Nashville: Bad Neighbors Music, 2009).
8. Riley Etheridge, Jr., *Powder Keg* (Nashville: Rock Ridge Music, 2011).
9. Riley Etheridge, Jr., *Better Days* EP (Nashville: Rock Ridge Music, Jan. 24, 2012).
10. Riley Etheridge Jr., *The Arrogance of Youth* (Nashville: Rock Ridge Music, Sept. 18, 2012).
11. Riley Etheridge, Jr., *The Straight and Narrow Way* (Nashville: Rock Ridge Music, 2014).
12. Riley Etheridge, Jr., *Secrets, Hope & Waiting* (Nashville: Rock Ridge Music, 2016).
13. Riley Etheridge, Jr., "Second Chance, Saving Grace," in *The Straight and Narrow Way* (Nashville: Rock Ridge Music, 2014).

Spoke 15—Prioritize Personal Growth: Enlightening Expansion

1. Gregg Levoy, *Callings: Finding and Following an Authentic Life* (New York: Three Rivers Press, 1997), 264.
2. Viktor E. Frankl, *Man's Search for Meaning* (Boston: Beacon Press, 2006), 113.
3. Richard Branson, "My Top 10 Quotes on Change," accessed on February 10, 2019, https://www.virgin.com/richard-branson/my-top-10-quotes-on-change.

4. Adelaide Anne Procter, *Legends and Lyrics, Part 1: A Legend of Provence* (Scotts Valley, CA: CreateSpace Independent Publishing Platform, 2016), line 284.

5. "Jim Rohn," Jim Rohn Official Facebook, June 20, 2013, https://www.facebook.com/OfficialJimRohn/posts/10152894778925635.

6. Gregg Levoy, *Callings: Finding and Following an Authentic Life* (New York: Three Rivers Press, 1997).

7. Gregg Levoy, *Vital Signs: The Nature and Nurture of Passion* (New York: Penguin, 2014).

8. Chip Conley, *PEAK: How Great Companies Get Their Mojo from Maslow* (San Francisco: Jossey-Bass/Wiley, 2007).

9. Chip Conley, *Emotional Equations: Simple Steps for Creating Happiness + Success in Business and Life* (New York: Atria/Simon & Schuster, 2012).

10. Chip Conley, *Wisdom @ Work: The Making of a Modern Elder* (New York: Currency/Crown Publishing Group, 2018).

Spoke 16—Connect to a Higher Power: Plugging in for Increased Wattage

1. Dalai Lama and Desmond Tutu with Douglas Abrams, *The Book of Joy: Lasting Happiness in a Changing World* (New York: Penguin Random House, 2016), 22.

2. Rabbi Rami Shapiro, "My Morning Ritual," *Spirituality and Health Magazine*, April 16, 2014, https://spiritualityhealth.com/articles/2014/04/16/rami-morning.

3. Jack Kornfield, "A Meditation on Lovingkindness," JackKornfield.com, accessed December 10, 2018, https://jackkornfield.com/meditation-lovingkindness/.

4. Spirit Rock Meditation Center, "Introduction to Buddhism: The Buddha's Story," adapted from *Teachings of the Buddha*, edited by Jack Kornfield with Gil Fronsdal (Boulder, CO: Shambhala, 2012), https://www.spiritrock.org/intro-to-buddhism.

5. Jai Uttal, "What is Kirtan?" jaiuttal.com, accessed December 10, 2018, http://www.jaiuttal.com/what-is-kirtan/.

Spoke 17—Craft Self-Expression: Igniting Your Inner Muse

1. Mary Oliver, *New and Selected Poems Volume One* (Boston: Beacon Books, 1992), 110.

2. Julia Cameron, *The Artist's Way: A Spiritual Path to Higher Creativity* (New York: Penguin Random House, 2016), iBooks version, 218.
3. Janine Willis and Alexander Todorov, "First Impressions: Making Up Your Mind After a 100-Ms Exposure to a Face," *Psychological Science* 17, no. 7 (July 2006), https://journals.sagepub.com/doi/10.1111/j.1467-9280.2006.01750.x.
4. Kim Rochelle Todd, Instagram, @kimrochelletodd.

Spoke 18—Create Intimacy: Inspiration for Love

1. Don Miguel Ruiz, *The Mastery of Love: A Practical Guide to the Art of Relationship* (California: Amber-Allen Publishing, 1999), xiii.
2. Matthew Kelly, *The Seven Levels of Intimacy: The Art of Loving and the Joy of Being Loved* (Boston: Beacon Publishing, 2005), 54.
3. Gary Chapman, *The 5 Love Languages: The Secret to Love that Lasts* (Chicago: Northfield Publishing, 2010), 15.
4. Ruiz, *The Mastery of Love*, 158.
5. Ruiz, *The Mastery of Love*, 187.

Conclusion: Putting It All Together in Your Up-Leveled Life

1. Carl Gustav Jung, Herbert Reed, Michael Scott Montague Fordham, Gerhard Adler, *The Collected Works of C.G. Jung: Psychology and Alchemy* (Princeton, NJ: Princeton University Press, 2014), Paragraph 208.

ACKNOWLEDGMENTS

I have always craved living an extraordinary life. The more wisdom I gather, the more I understand that an extraordinary life is inspired by not only who you are as a person, but also by those who surround you on your journey.

I want to express my deepest gratitude to my Exceptional Executives, whom I interviewed in their corporate headquarters, homes, and everywhere in between; their personal stories amplify our message about well-being and success, and their distinct approaches are changing the way our corporate and entrepreneurial communities recognize outstanding leadership: John Mackey, Denise Brosseau, John Worden, May Lindstrom, Kara Goldin, Yanik Silver, Rich Fernandez, Marie Case, Steven Rice, Judy Belk, Robyn Denholm, Gopi Kallayil, Jen Groover, Riley Etheridge, Chip Conley, Angela Macke, Kim Todd, and Scott Kucirek. I can't thank you all enough for your trust.

Thank you to my beloved girls, Madeline and Amelia. Having you both in my life- exactly as you are- is my greatest joy. Your presence in our home sanctuary, your support of every project I have ever undertaken, and your astonishing awareness of love, truth, and the goal of happiness inspires me with awe. Remember that your power lies in the intersection of your unique talents, and what the world needs. You are my greatest teachers.

I am fortunate to have had mentors that have had a profound impact on my life, and in every way, are extraordinary themselves. I am thankful that my parents instilled in me a reverence for education, a belief in the importance of motivation, and the desire for giving back. When I was in high school, Gary Fountain shared his vision for my potential, and even today (maybe over falafel in NYC!), I owe so much of my joie de vivre and success to his brilliant example. Riley Etheridge, who shaped my early corporate career with unstoppable encouragement, remains one of my most inspired connections. My primary spiritual teacher, Sharon Wilson, with her uber-intuition, has helped me up-level everything I want to manifest for myself.

Steve Harrison's priceless time and talent helped me shape my initial ideas for this book into true wisdom, and his Quantum Leap Program provided just the community I needed. Denise Brosseau's early thought leadership advice set me sailing. Patty Aubrey's open heart and key connections created a cascade of magic. Sam Horn's authentic encouragement for my writing and her public speaking savvy for my keynotes continues to carry me along like a river. Thank you to the special, bold members of Maverick1000, who have inspired me further to build out an impact business as well as a movement that will change our workforce for the better. You all showed up at just the perfect time.

I deeply value my incredible agent, Marilyn Allen, of Allen O'Shea Literary Agency, who believed in me instantly, and knew, without a doubt, that this book would find the perfect home. I want to give my deepest thanks and a group hug to my outstanding publishing team at Nicholas Brealey Publishing/ Hachette UK. Thank you to my editor, Alison Hankey, who clearly saw the vision from the start; to my production manager, Michelle Morgan, who kept us on track; and to Head of Sales Melissa Carl. I am in awe, still, of the show-stopping cover design by rockstar, London-based graphic designer Aaron Munday of 12 Orchards. Thank you to my first editor, Debby Englander, who helped me shape my passion into a book proposal; to my PR agent, Tess Woods, for your research and tireless work at getting our message out; and to my unstoppable and audacious marketing team, led by Mike Cline, the CEO of Tech Guys Who Get Marketing, alongside Shelby Larson and Addison Clearwood. With you all, the tides have beautifully risen.

I acknowledge with the deepest gratitude that I have outstanding medical care. With my health regained, some of these doctors have gloriously "discharged me from care," but I will never forget their excellence: Andrew Gross, MD, Chief, Rheumatology Clinic at UCSF Health; Kerry

Cho, MD, Nephrologist, UCSF Heath, and before these two superstars: Johnathan Graf, MD at UCSF Rheumatology and Pedram Fatehi, MD at Stanford Nephrology. My oncology surgeon, Sima Porten, MD, UCSF Dept of Urology, swooped in like an angel when I needed her most. My first alternative medicine doctor, Rick McKinney, MD at USCF, set me on a healing path and my alternative medicine and cancer prevention specialist, Bita Badakshan, MD at the Center for New Medicine, ushered me into truly vibrant health and continues to up-level everything I know about healing.

People say that your friends say a lot about who you are. I could not have written this book and undertaken this life mission without their support. Mollie McNealy Sciascia, my incredible sister, is the most beautiful soul; I have been privileged to walk alongside her every year of this lifetime. Kee-Ann Batory, thank you, goddess, for every bit of loyalty and encouragement; my life was blessed the day I met you at Esalen. Marguerite Havlis, my soul-sister and my decades-long friend, you continue to lift my spirit (and carry Birdie's torch) from Tucson. Michelle Arpin-Begina, with our twin paths on separate coasts, we continue to forge our extraordinary ideas (while on spa retreats no less!) and stretch what is possible. Thank you, Brenda Reynolds, for helping me see this project from start to finish, and for becoming a lifelong friend along the way.

Lastly, I want to thank God, my spirit guides, my guardian angels, the gods and goddesses, my highest self, my soul's purpose, and any other exceptional, unseen magic that has touched me, that changed the course of my unbelievable challenges, allowed me not only to live but to *thrive*, and that, no doubt, has gently nudged me to step it up and to serve.

INDEX